THE GROWING
LOCAL CHURCH

THE GROWING LOCAL CHURCH

Donald J. MacNair

A CANON PRESS BOOK
BAKER BOOK HOUSE • Grand Rapids, Michigan

© 1975 by Baker Book House Company
ISBN: 0-8010-5983-6
Printed in the United States of America

DEDICATED

to

EVELYN

whose love is part of my ministry

and

whose commitment to Christ
enabled me to do the extensive
traveling necessary to develop
this material "on the field."

Contents

sion: A Declaration of Specific Purpose • Benefits of the Declaration of Specific Purpose • Analyzing the Statement of Principle • The Congregation Must Know Itself Before Proceeding • "Community" and Evangelism Related • An Example of One Church's Answers to the Questions Pinpointing the Three Key Truths • Drafting the Statement of Principle • The Previous Example Synthesized • Preparing to Draft the Statements Concerning the Factors of Influence • Guidelines for the Committee • Step-by-Step Analysis • Building and Grounds • Completion and Adoption of a Statement

APPENDICES

LIST OF CHARTS

Preface

Christians belong to churches. Because they are members of the body of Christ by virtue of his redeeming grace in their lives, they are members of *the* church, the invisible church. But Christianity is not an "existence in a vacuum." Each Christian needs the special work of the Holy Spirit found in communion, fellowship, and blessing from other Christians, and likewise each Christian needs the experience of sharing himself with other Christians. Therefore, Christians belong to local congregations, to branches of the visible church.

Yet all too often a particular church fails to be all that the Bible seems to imply it ought to be. Once in a while we encounter a church that seems to be "with it," a church that has meaningful worship, a well-balanced overall ministry, obvious concern for each other, and a vital concern to present Christ to the lost. One way to describe such a church is that it is "growing up."

This book is a study of what makes such a church "tick."

Two doctrines are absolutely fundamental to any such study—the doctrine of the verbal inspiration[1] of the Bible and the doctrine of the church. The doctrine of the verbal inspiration of the Bible is basic because the evangelical church claims to be developed directly upon the Bible. If there is no assurance that the Bible is indeed verbally inspired and therefore infallible, then there is no assurance that a church developed on it will even have the potential of becoming a "growing" church. Not only that, but there can be no middle ground on the doctrine of verbal inspiration. Either the Bible is verbally inspired or it isn't. Any equivoca-

---

1. Verbal inspiration is not to be confused with a heretical theory of inspiration called the "mechanical dictation theory." A good definition of verbal inspiration is "that God superintended the very choice of words in the Holy Volume so that it may be truly said to be entirely God's Word without admixture of human error" (R. Laird Harris, *Inspiration and Canonicity of the Bible* [Zondervan, 1957], p. 20).

tion about this doctrine invites heresy and, eventually, apostasy even from well-meaning evangelicals. Therefore, if the Bible is verbally inspired, it stands as the final authority for the life of the church and of its members. This authority is to be maintained even if our feelings might seem to point in another direction.

The doctrine of the church is important because the Bible declares that the visible church will exist until the Lord returns. By comparing Scripture with Scripture, I will demonstrate in chapter 1 that the church described in the Bible is both indestructible and indispensable. Contemporary events show that the evangelical church is very much alive today and still growing. In a feature article in the *St. Louis Globe Democrat* (February 23, 1974) entitled "Clergy: Supply vs. Demand," Dr. Robert G. Rayburn, president of Covenant Theological Seminary, corroborates this: "The evangelical seminary has far more demands from churches than people to supply them."

Students of contemporary theology all agree that these two doctrines are at the root of just about every theological discussion and development today. This book is written on two premises related to these doctrines:

1. It is unashamedly committed to the doctrine of the verbal inspiration of the Bible and to the indestructibility and indispensability of the visible church.
2. It attempts to elucidate the fundamental biblical principles upon which a church functions and about which the people maintain their relationships. Further, it attempts to do this about each major facet of the life of the church that seeks to "grow up." Finally, since these concepts are derived from the Bible, it unashamedly commits all these functions and relationships, and, of course, the people themselves, to subjection under the headship of Jesus Christ.

This book reflects my method of using the Bible as the source for developing and nurturing the contemporary church. That is:

- no concept or its application in developing a church may be in contradiction to anything revealed in the Bible;
- where the Bible gives specific principles on which to proceed, the church's concepts and their application must be in conformity with the Bible;
- where the Bible does not give specific principles on which to proceed, the church's concepts and their application must be in substantial agreement with and logically proceed from whatever degree of revelation the Bible does make.

This book, therefore, sets forth concepts for church development even when their application may be contrary to many of the popular, contemporary practices of the church.

Further, I have written the book on the premise that it is necessary to apply these concepts in some detail and in practical ways. Therefore I have attempted to:

- apply them to the major areas of the church and also to the subordinate facets of the major areas
- enhance with practical illustrations the discussion of how to apply these concepts
- supply occasional supporting arguments to encourage churches to pay the price of applying them
- supply occasional warnings of pitfalls and discouragements that could undermine and destroy the unity and vitality of a church if it fails to pay the price of applying these concepts, or if it tries to take shortcuts in doing so

This is a book that flows from a ministry of twenty-eight years of in-depth experience with churches in various stages of development and growth. It is in four parts. Part 1 presents the basic concepts of a biblical church. It demonstrates the Bible's clear distinction between men's organizations for religious purposes and the true church, under the headship of Christ, with both organization and organism working together for the glory of God. It is in this discussion that I have attempted to conceptualize the resources and functions of a church, and the relationships between the functions themselves and the functions and the resources. This conceptualization is used as a basis for several in-depth discussions later in the book, particularly in chapter 12.

Part 2 deals with both the office and work of the pastor-teacher. It takes into account the tensions and fears felt by many ministers, especially seminary students, concerning the nonbiblical demands that evangelicals often put on the pastor. It describes the components of the so-called job description of the pastor and relates them to biblical concepts. Possibly the most important emphasis of this entire section is on the authority-base from which the pastor-teacher ministers. This authority-base is defined as the pastor's responsibility as a ruler over the souls of the flock given to his charge. By "ruler," I mean, of course, one who by loving persuasion, admonition, and example, not autocratic power, motivates the flock. By this I also mean that the pastor-teacher is one among the other elders who must give an account to God for the lives of the flock.

11

I have also provided a practical chapter entitled "Potpourri of the Pastor's Office." The concepts for the pastor's office will have been discussed in the preceding chapters. Yet many pastorates, fully oriented to biblical concepts, can only be described as failures. Knowing how and when to use "sanctified common sense" often is the difference between success and failure. This chapter is therefore a composite of experience given as advice for the pastor.

Part 3 treats both the offices and work of the various church officials. The New Testament terms "elder" and "deacon" are defined and used throughout the discussion. The lack of intrinsic biblical authority for the office of "trustee" is examined. Finally, the unique value of each office is interrelated with that of the others. The study of the work of the elder and of the deacon is the most basic material of this section; it is supported by extensive practical applications and presumes that both are indeed high offices that demand spiritual commitment.

Part 4 deals with the "people," the congregation. In matters of business it deals with them as the corporation. It is in Part 4 that I develop the concept of a specific purpose for each church. My practice of unifying a local congregation around a specific purpose developed between 1955 and 1956. Since this is a unique presentation, a word about my personal experience seems in order. I had already been in the ministry about ten years when one day, in God's providence, seven men stood around my desk burdened with the thought of establishing a Christian college and seminary.[2] This commitment soon became a factor in my own congregation's life because the campus was to be located less than a mile from the church building. The challenges of having a college and seminary on the doorstep of the local congregation soon had to be met. For instance, we had to find places of service for college and seminary students and their wives, and for faculty members and their wives, while not depriving the original church members of their necessary responsibility to share their gifts and talents. Another challenge, by far more personal to me, was to learn how to benefit from criticisms of theological students. Anyone who has ever worked with those particular young men will probably agree that they are the world's most critical church members. (My wife, by the way, was the key I needed to deal with this challenge. Just about every time I was ready to give up, she patiently reminded me of our

---

2. The schools became Covenant College in Lookout Mountain, Tennessee, and Covenant Theological Seminary in Saint Louis, Missouri.

12

early married life—when she was married to just such a "world's worst!")

Little by little these challenges were met. First, the elders and I made broad policy decisions that enabled the church to continue moving ahead. We also sought to define the problems each challenge brought with it and to propose solutions that were adequate for each need and were related to other solutions. The ultimate result of this experience was the development of a church program that kept the life of the church unified while incorporating a new dimension. It became evident that we had found a direction for the church that I later called a specific purpose of this church.

Still another personal experience affected my development of this idea. In 1964 the Lord led me into the full-time ministry of establishing new churches. Within a few years a pattern began to emerge. That pattern was that, given boundaries of church government and doctrine, there actually *was no pattern!* Each set of people, bringing their own experiences, prejudices, and aspirations with them, having various degrees of growth in Christ, meeting in temporary quarters, representing vastly different communities even in the same embryonic group, had to be helped as a special and unique mission church.

It is evident that just as I developed a de facto specific purpose in 1955-56, many individual churches have done the same. I have been gratified to find that this concept is at work throughout the church of Jesus Christ. I have learned of some churches that actually started out with a specific purpose in order to minister to their changing communities. I have also learned that, although many churches have approximately the same specific purpose as other churches, the soul-searching necessary to determine the final direction for each church is the price that must be paid in order to make the application of a specific purpose real and not simply academic.

The "nuts and bolts" of church programs are described in Part 4. In these discussions no attempt is made to present an exhaustive study. Rather, the presentation of concepts and their application has been the guiding principle, although one or two of the topics seem to demand and hence are given an extended discussion.

The material in this book is most directly applicable to churches with up to four or five hundred people. This is the size church in which I have direct experience. The ways and means of applying this material to larger churches are not difficult to project, but I have not done it in the text.

Writing this book has been both exciting and exhausting. It is a sequel to my text on establishing churches, *The Birth, Care, and Feeding of a Local Church* (Canon Press, 1973), and provides material for the continued nourishment of a local church after it has been established.

Part 1
BASIC CONCEPTS OF THE LOCAL CHURCH

1
Basic Concepts
of the Local Church

Everyone is familiar with a food store. We use the corner grocery or major food chain supermarket again and again until we know the arrangement of food on the shelves. But few patrons know much about the myriad services and activities needed to keep food stores going. Regular church goers, too, know a lot about their church—or at least about the arrangement of people in the pews. But few really know "what makes it tick."

So the place to start this study of a church that is really "growing up" is the definition of the local church—not just a simple two- or three-line abstract from theological textbooks, but a vital, comprehensive, meaty expression that is so real it can be tasted.[1]

Definition: The Viable Local Church

A statement defining the church must encompass the members, their relationship to the corporate body, their purpose for joining in the corporate body, and the purpose of the corporate body itself. Following this criterion as an outline, the definition can be developed further:

The viable local church is a body of believers (Ephesians 1:22-23; 2:20-22). This means:

(a) The church, regardless of its factor of growth, will constantly strive to receive into membership only those who have a credible confession of faith, particularly credible evidence that they are indeed born again and that their lives are reflecting the fruit of the Holy Spirit.

---

1. In this preliminary definition, no attempt will be made to relate each detail of the basic concepts presented to a Scripture passage. As these concepts recur throughout the book the scriptural references and discussions of them will be made.

(b) The church will not deny membership to a believer on the grounds of social, racial, or even varying theological views so long as the candidate sincerely commits himself to be under the discipline of the church officers.

(c) The church, simply because it is a "body of believers," will be an "organization," that is, "the systematic union of individuals in a body whose officers, agents, and members work together for a common end."

(d) Simultaneously, the church will be an organism, that is, "a body composed of different organs or parts performing special functions that are mutually dependent and essential to life."

The viable local church is a necessity for the believer. The implications of this statement are:

(a) The church is indispensable. The Bible teaches (Ephesians 3:10 and 5:27) that the purpose of God was to bring glory to himself by the evidence of his wisdom and power in redeeming a bride (not *many* individual brides) for Christ.

The Bible teaches (Ephesians 4:16) that for the individual believer to be personally and entirely fulfilled he needs to share in the blessings of graces and gifts given to other believers. For instance, worship must have a corporate aspect as well as an individual aspect: there is a blessing in corporate singing that a person singing by himself just cannot have. Fellowship is another instance. The value of subjection and discipline is also less without the corporate whole. The need for corporate prayer demands the body of Christ, as does the need for instruction in truth and application of it.

(b) The church is indestructible. In one way or another the visible church will exist until the return of Christ (I Corinthians 11:26). Not only that, it must continue to exist since it is indispensable. Consider that it is the church that will stand against the gates of hell all through history; that the entire church is necessary to make the sacraments fully meaningful to each individual over a long period of time; and that the need for Christian examples and training will always exist and will be met through the organized utilization of the gifts of the various members, all of which are necessary for this fulfillment. Furthermore, the only way the believer can fully obey the Great Commission is to be

18

involved in a ministry from which a local church actually comes into existence.[2]

The viable local church simultaneously maintains three standards for the benefit of the believers: the preaching and teaching of the entire counsel of God, and from the entire Bible; the proper administration of the sacraments; and the proper administration of spiritual oversight and discipline throughout the congregation.[3] The implications of this statement are:

(a) Since every evangelical church automatically has a doctrinal preference, its confession will be the church's basic doctrinal standard for faith and practice. It thus will dictate both the direction and the limiting boundaries of the church's unique ministry in its community. The purpose of the church (reconciliation of man to God and all the implications thereof)[4] is comprehended under this standard and therefore becomes basic to the preaching and teaching referred to in this discussion.

(b) Since every church automatically has a governmental preference, its application of this standard will determine the degree of each individual's responsibility for and to the corporate body, and the degree of discipline exercised by the corporate body over the individual member.

(c) The church must have generated a tangible degree of commitment and loyalty to it from individual members who demonstrate their attitudes by such things as willingness to submit to the discipline of their brethren.

(d) The church must have the maturity and commitment necessary to evaluate regularly and in depth its effectiveness in accomplishing its biblical purpose and to pay the price of consequent adjustment in order to accomplish its purpose. This especially challenges the ability to keep all these standards operative at the same time.

The viable local church has the primary responsibility for maintaining its three basic standards as the task of the organism (not to be confused with organization) itself (Ephesians 4:11-16). This means:

(a) Church officership is not merely a complimentary honor.

---

2. Cf. *The Birth, Care, and Feeding of a Local Church*, p. 2.
3. Ibid.
4. Ibid., chap. 2.

19

(b) Church membership is not merely an organizational function. It is a vital part of the organism itself. The officers are themselves parts of the body, as are the members. Except in matters of judicial discipline and spiritual oversight, everything the officers do means planning and programming for their own benefit as well as for the benefit to the entire church. All of it also needs their personal participation as much as the participation of other members. Hence the officers work as part of the organism, not as an external organizational authority;

(c) It is the existence of organism, not mere organization, that binds together the body of Christ. "Instead, speaking the truth in love, we will in all things grow up into him who is the Head, that is, Christ. From him the whole body, *joined and held together by every supporting ligament,* grows and builds itself up in love, as each part does its work" (Ephesians 4:15-16).[5]

(d) Organization is primarily the tool necessary to define and limit the proper working relationships of the members of the organization.

(e) The organism concept of the church enables all new members to be accepted as integral parts of the whole body and to enable it immediately to benefit by the contributions of new members through their particular gifts, regardless of their degree of doctrinal sophistication. Also, it enables the long-standing members to contribute to the new member.

(f) For churches with a denominational relationship, the other churches, officers, or hierarchy have some responsibility for defining standards for the local government, for operating these standards, and for hearing appeals from those disagreeing with the application of the standards on the local level.

The viable local church is a body of believers in which the ways and means of function between the members, the pastor, and the officers has been delineated (e.g., Acts 20:28). The implications involved in this statement are:

(a) The church has a distinctive constitution and bylaws.

(b) It is biblical to have a ruling and teaching elder who normally is employed full time by the church. (Recently this premise has been under increasing scrutiny by sincere Chris-

---

5. This statement will be dealt with at length in Part 4.

tians who conclude that all the functions of the pastor are also assigned to the ruling elder, with the consequence that the separate office of pastor is unbiblical; this will be dealt with in Part 2.)

(c) Membership is vital to the church and implies positive involvement in the ministry of the church and willing subjection to oversight by the elders.

(d) Potential members should have some training and orientation before being admitted to membership.

(e) The constitution (essentially, the unchanging principles of the church) and the bylaws (essentially, the rather elastic application of these principles to the "nitty-gritty" working of the congregation) reflect the "personality" of the church.

(f) The bylaws are constantly evaluated and refined to keep the thrust of the constitution in a contemporary mold.

(g) The "charter" of the corporation (trusteeship)[6] is purely a civil instrument which does not control the ecclesiastical posture of the church.

(h) None of these documents is permitted to stand unilaterally.

(i) The constitution's statement of purpose (including its statement of specific purpose, which will be discussed in Part 4) will be the focus about which all the functioning of the church is oriented.

A summary definition of the viable local church, therefore, might go like this:

A body of believers, committed to each other for fulfillment and out of necessity, in the midst of whom the whole counsel of God, from the whole Bible, is faithfully preached and taught, the sacraments and discipline are properly administered, and the relationship between members, pastor, and officers has been established.

Fundamental Resources upon Which
Every Viable Local Church
Must Be Developed

The four fundamental resources upon which every viable local church must be developed are:

6. See footnote 1, p. 120

- the headship of Christ,
- the final authority of the Bible for all of our faith and our practice,
- the work of the Holy Spirit,
- the eldership providing spiritual oversight.

The Headship of Christ: "And God placed all things under his feet and appointed him to be head over everything for the church, which is his body, the fullness of him who fills everything in every way" (Ephesians 1:22-23).

This truth is so thoroughly treated in every worthwhile theological textbook that only enough mention of it is needed here to make it dramatically clear. Christ's headship is, of course, for the glory of the Father.

Much to the amazement and even chagrin of many contemporary evangelical church members, no church in reality is a democracy. True, churches often determine solutions to local circumstances on the premise that "the majority vote rules." Yet, if that method is used for anything of principle, the church is in violation of the Scriptures. The church is under a King: it is a Kingdom. The King—King Jesus, as the Scottish Covenanters called him—is the absolute potentate of the church, whether today's churchmen admit it or not! His commands, therefore, are not merely altruistic theorizing, nor merely sincere motivational devices; they are orders (note John 13:34)! The impact of this fact occurs when the Christian realizes that he must some day stand before King Jesus and give an account of the way he obeyed those orders (II Corinthians 5:10)!

The Final Authority of the Bible: "And how from infancy you have known the holy Scriptures, which are able to make you wise for salvation through faith in Christ Jesus. All Scripture is God-breathed and is useful for teaching, rebuking, correcting and training in righteousness" (2 Timothy 3:15-16).

Experience demonstrates that most Christians will readily agree to this premise, yet often do not want to accept the consequences of a firm commitment to it. When they "feel good" about this or that person, doctrine, practice, or institution, they find it difficult to submit their will to a final authority—the Bible—if that means disregarding their good feelings. But once the Christian dilutes the authority of the Bible with his own "good feelings," the wedge of unbelief has been driven into that individual's heart. The most heinous wedge is the warm response so often given to a sincere

22

preacher or scholar (sincere, yes, but sincerely wrong!) who questions the full verbal inspiration of the entire Bible in its original autographs. That wedge has inevitably led person after person and church after church away from Jesus Christ as God incarnate.

The Work of the Holy Spirit: "In him the whole building is joined together and rises to become a holy temple in the Lord. And in him you too are being built together to become a dwelling in which God lives by his Spirit" (Ephesians 2:21-22).

The third resource for developing the church is God the Holy Spirit. It is he who indwells each believer, dwells in the midst of the believers, and builds them together into the "living-stone" house of God. It is the work of the Holy Spirit that provides each church with the gifts it needs for its specific ministry. No church can even pretend to be a viable local church if it has everything and lacks the ministry of the Holy Spirit.

The Spiritual Oversight of the Eldership: "Obey your leaders and submit to their authority. They keep watch over you as men who must give an account. Obey them so that their work will be a joy, not a burden, for that would be of no advantage to you" (Hebrews 13:17).

The elders of the church serve in a place of responsibility which is both different from the first three resources and yet, by the decree of God, also essential for the church's existence. Jesus Christ and the Holy Spirit are God, the same in substance, equal in power and glory. The Bible is the verbally inspired revelation by God of himself, showing man what he should believe about God and what he should do about that belief. The elders, on the other hand, are like all other members of the church, merely sinners saved by grace. If the standard were intrinsic merit, the elders could not even be considered resources to the church.

However, God has decreed that there is to be a church conducted in a decent and orderly way under the leadership and governing restraint of men specially gifted and supplied by him as his gifts to the church, and he has charged these men (under ordination oath) to give a meaningful account to him of each of the sheep over which they were charged with responsibility. In this sense, the elders are indeed a necessary resource to the church. (The first three resources have been discussed in many worthwhile theological textbooks and will not be treated at length here. However, the subject of elders and their oversight will be developed throughout the book.)

The Church Itself—the Corporate Body of Believers—Is More Important Than Its Individual Members and Officers

The church is not a building. Nor is it merely an ecclesiastical organization. The church, as defined earlier, is the body of believers. Therefore, the church is more important than individuals (including the pastor and elders), more important than plans and programs, and certainly more important than buildings. This premise is absolute and unchanging. Accepted as such, it can be the turning point for resolving many "sticky" and difficult decisions. This premise demands much of the corporate body of believers. The congregation must understand itself well enough to "spell out" its personality so that all of its plans, programs, and personnel can be oriented toward developing that particular church to the fullest possible extent.

Further, it is clear that the elders of the church must continue to be participants in the congregation even while exercising their responsibility of eldership. Such verses as Acts 20:28 indicate that their responsibility is to lead the flock, feed the flock, be an example to the flock, and restrain the flock. Far too often the elders fall into the trap of serving their church by "setting policy and making decisions" once a month with little involvement between times. Often, they simply depend on the pastor and even hold him solely accountable for the welfare of the church except where discipline is demanded. In essence they have structured an old-fashioned, almost military, "chain of command" administration for the church.

The Functions Which Must Always Be Active in Every Viable Local Church

The viable local church, then, is a marvelous structure in which God dwells (Ephesians 1:22-23). Its resources, functions (which have not yet been delineated, of course), and their relationships all fit together into a unified whole—a unit, if you will. By synthesizing the foregoing material, it can be seen that the functions a church must have are:

- worship, including, of course, the sacraments;
- growth in grace, including instruction, sanctification (and therefore discipline), and fellowship;

24

- outreach, including evangelism, missions, and community involvement;
- acts of mercy, including the diaconate and community and world concerns.

Each of these functions is under the spiritual oversight of the elders, yet the elders themselves must be involved in them for their own spiritual benefit and contribution. And, all are for the glory of the Father.

Safeguard for the Future of the Church

It is often stated that no church will ever survive the inroads of liberalism and heresy. This is not necessarily true. The truth is that no church has a guarantee that it will never fall prey to this device of Satan. No matter how carefully the constitution is originally written and how sincere the people are, no guarantee exists. Righteousness cannot be achieved either by legislation or by sincerity. However, the Bible provides a built-in safeguard to maintain a church true to the Lord: the ruling elder. The key is that *before* he is ordained and installed he must demonstrate that the biblical qualifications are in fact present in his life, and, further, *before* ordination and installation he must be sufficiently trained in the doctrine, government, and work of his church so that he can take an intelligent oath of ordination; and finally, *before* he is ordained and installed he must be committed to giving the necessary time that his work will require of him. Actually, the strength and caliber of the first body of officers does much to determine the strength and caliber of the succeeding bodies of officers. However, an existing eldership can indeed upgrade its caliber if the basic qualifications for the office are present. In addition, each body of officers, regardless of its individual or corporate caliber, must constantly be growing in the Lord. With this safeguard, the spiritual future of the church is potentially assured.

Deacons—The Ministry of Mercy and Service

In many evangelical churches today the deacons function in a banker-usher-caretaker syndrome. In some places, the diaconate's only saving virtue is that it is a prerequisite to becoming an elder, although it rarely provides any training for the office. Actually, the deacons have a marvelous calling for service and consequently

25

a responsibility for an outreach of mercy to the church family and beyond to the community. They may be assigned other duties. Unless they are actively at work in their basic area of service, however, the church will lack a major ministry needed to keep the organism functioning with vital life.

The Viable Local Church Conceptualized

Figure 1 is a conceptualization of the local church which illustrates these resources, functions, and their relationships. The illustration has a threefold purpose: to show (a) that all the various resources and functions must be operative simultaneously, (b) that there indeed is a relationship between the resources and the functions of each church that must be maintained, and (c) to enable the reader more easily and more permanently to see the church for what it is.

Conclusion

The *ecclesia,* the "called-out ones," the church, is both indispensable and indestructible. Yet, any given local church, if it is to be viable, cannot content itself to be a body of believers staunchly declaring these truths. To be viable, each local church must relate the concepts described above to the specific circumstances of its existence. And, as children grow, as people move away while others come into the church, as neighborhoods change, relating these concepts to the church becomes a constant, necessary task for the church. The viable church, then, is one which has the eternal, unchanging message and which pays the price successfully to communicate to contemporary man.

THE LOCAL CHURCH CONCEPTUALIZED

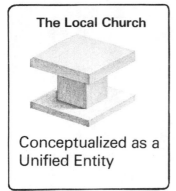

The Local Church

Conceptualized as a
Unified Entity

Artwork by Greg McNair

A.

G. C. H.
D.
F.
E.

B.

THE RESOURCES AND FUNCTIONS OF THE LOCAL CHURCH AND THE RELATIONSHIP BETWEEN THEM

LEGEND

RESOURCES:
A. Jesus Christ, Head of the Church, for God the Father.
B. The Bible, the Authority—base on which the Church is built.
C. The Holy Spirit, fitting the Church together.
D. The Elders, providing spiritual oversight.

RELATIONSHIP:
Based on the Bible and the work and persons of
Jesus Christ and the Holy Spirit, the Eldership both:
1. Oversee each Function of the Church
2. Participate in each Function
all for the glory of God the Father.

FUNCTIONS:
E. Worship
F. Growth in Grace:
  • Instruction
  • Sanctification
  • Fellowship
G. Acts of Mercy:
  • Diaconate
  • Community and
    World concern
H. Outreach:
  • Evangelism
  • Missions
  • Community involvement

FIGURE 1

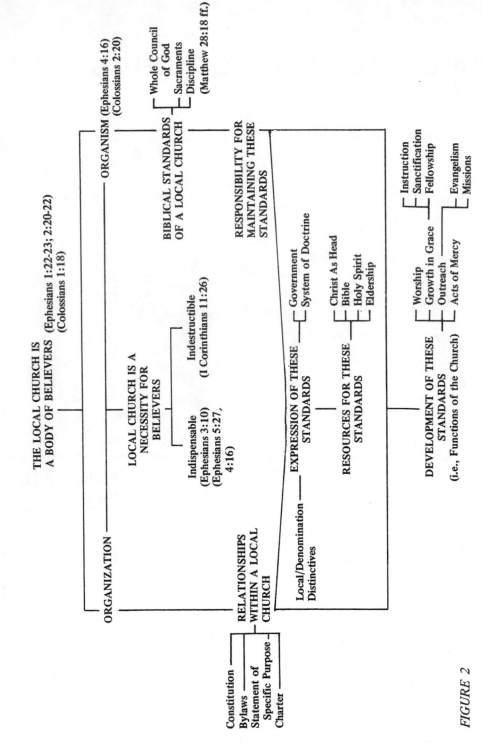

THE LOCAL CHURCH IS
A BODY OF BELIEVERS (Ephesians 1:22-23; 2:20-22)
(Colossians 1:18)

ORGANIZATION

ORGANISM (Ephesians 4:16)
(Colossians 2:20)

LOCAL CHURCH IS A
NECESSITY FOR
BELIEVERS

Indispensable
(Ephesians 3:10)
(Ephesians 5:27,
4:16)

Indestructible
(I Corinthians 11:26)

BIBLICAL STANDARDS
OF A LOCAL CHURCH

Whole Council
of God
Sacraments
Discipline
(Matthew 28:18 ff.)

RELATIONSHIPS
WITHIN A LOCAL
CHURCH

Constitution
Bylaws
Statement of
Specific Purpose
Charter

EXPRESSION OF THESE
STANDARDS

Local/Denomination
Distinctives

Government
System of Doctrine

RESPONSIBILITY FOR
MAINTAINING THESE
STANDARDS

RESOURCES FOR THESE
STANDARDS

Christ As Head
Bible
Holy Spirit
Eldership

DEVELOPMENT OF THESE
STANDARDS
(i.e., Functions of the Church)

Worship
Growth in Grace
Outreach
Acts of Mercy

Instruction
Sanctification
Fellowship

Evangelism
Missions

FIGURE 2

28

Part 2
THE PASTOR-TEACHER

2

The Pastor: A Prophet
Called by God

"God called me into the ministry almost three years ago. At that time he showed me that the most important activity of my life was to share with others the joy of the Lord. I've preached and witnessed every chance I had while in seminary, and it's always been great. In fact, if it hadn't been for that, I probably would have quit 'sem' long ago. Then, a few weeks ago I went to a church as a pastoral candidate. As I listened to what the elders thought I should do, I suddenly realized that most of my time would be spent in plain, old-fashioned business administration and in the work of promotion. They even would expect me to head up a building committee for a new church building. That's not what my call to the ministry is all about. I don't want to spend my life as a business administrator. So—I guess the pastorate is no place for me."

What a sad note on which to start this portion of the book. Yet the young man who told me this story and the church at which he was a candidate are far from the exceptional or even the occasional cases of nonbiblical concepts of the pastor and his work.

The Call to the Pastorate

Both seminary student and congregation alike must accept a fundamental aspect of God's work among men: he does indeed "call" men into the ministry! This call simultaneously keeps the minister humbled before the living God (even Paul claimed to be the vilest of sinners in God's sight—no room here for self-pride!) and responsible for proclaiming the Gospel. A supplementary benefit is the comforting assurance his call gives the minister when Satan tempts him with doubts about his "success" in the ministry. If being "called" seems old-fashioned—so be it! Paul specifically declares that God gives men "to be pastors and teachers" (Ephesians 4:11).

31

God's calling men is a much more fundamental premise for a successful ministry than normally realized. Since it is so basic, and since it is also absolutely necessary for a proper appreciation of the pastorate, a summary of its characteristics is in order. A pastor's calling is actually an integration of three separate callings of God on his life. In the first place, he is called by God from sin unto life: "Praise be to the God and Father of our Lord Jesus Christ, who has blessed us in the heavenly realms with every spiritual blessing in Christ. For he chose us in him before the creation of the world" (Ephesians 1:3-4a). "For those God foreknew he also predestined to be conformed to the likeness of his Son, that he might be the firstborn among many brothers. And those he predestined, he also called; those he called, he also justified; those he justified, he also glorified" (Romans 8:29-30). Almighty God called the pastor to himself without first demanding acts of worth as preconditions for acceptance. Nor did God act in response to divine awareness that eventually the pastor would want God to love him. Therefore, whatever else is developing in his life, the pastor is indeed a specific, a direct, a personal object of God's love and grace.

From this premise the second calling of the pastor comes into focus. It is a call by God into full employment in a specialized ministry, and because it is an undeniable call from God it must be a real thing to the minister, even though many today are discrediting its essentiality.

One prerequisite to this calling to a ministry is evidence of qualifications for eldership (1 Timothy 3; Titus 1), even though they may not be fully developed. The only ingredient that may safely be lacking is the spiritual maturity implied throughout these passages. Maturity demands time to have experienced the hand of the Lord in the course of living through circumstances which try one's faith. Even though a young man may not have had enough time to develop spiritual maturity, he obviously should begin his special theological training.

Another prerequisite is a compelling desire to be used by God in some aspects of the ministry, a desire which, by its presence, becomes one of the vehicles through which God confirms his calling to the heart of his child. For instance, when a candidate for the pastorate is only interested in teaching, but has no inclination to preach, counsel, lead, or serve, he ought to rethink his calling. It is hard to see how he is "desiring the office." A usual way in which God works is gradually to confirm his call upon his child as that Christian willingly serves to the best of his ability and availability wherever he is.

The third call is to a specific ministry. It has three component parts. The first is that the prospective pastor has satisfactorily mastered a thorough training and study program, all the while maintaining at least some active participation in the field of service for the Lord. Second, he has been examined by those with whom he will be a peer and found to have the biblical qualifications for the office, to be proficient enough to accept the responsibility of Christian service, side by side with them, and to have some evidence of the good hand of God upon him. Finally, a congregation of God's people has been persuaded that he is God's particular man for them and issued to him a call to become their pastor.[1]

This study of his "calling" demonstrates, therefore, that the question brought up by our young "sem" friend must be dealt with on the premise that it is a major and an eternal thing (cf. 1 Timothy 5:19). Neither he nor the church can brush aside the potential work of God in his life as having been a "mistake."

Administration in the Pastorate

The next question is: "What really is the biblical function of the man called to be a pastor?" Some of the work he must do is evident from the instructions given primarily to Timothy and Titus:

- be an example—1 Timothy 4:12-13
- defend the faith—1 Timothy 4:14-15
- preach the Word—2 Timothy 4:1-2
- discipline the flock—2 Timothy 4:1-2
- equip the saints for the work of service (including special areas of teaching)—Ephesians 4:11
- shepherd the flock—1 Peter 5:2; Ephesians 4:13-14
- use authority—Titus 2:15–3:2
- demonstrate self-control and self-guardianship—Acts 20:28

In the Ephesians 4:11 passage, Paul ties all these things together under a magnificent title—"pastor-teacher."

The problem the young seminarian faced was that these facets of his task seemed lost in the church's requirement to do other

---

1. Such a call might also come, for example, from a mission board or the armed services for the chaplaincy.

things. For instance, the following list is all too typical of the kind of things evangelical churches want their pastors to do:

- preach three times a week
- visit the sick
- visit every family of the congregation at least twice a year
- teach the adult class in Sunday School
- generally be responsible that the building and grounds are properly cared for, even on occasion filling in and doing things that have been overlooked by the members
- service most of the nitty-gritty programs of the church
- be prepared at least to arrange for, and possibly actually to furnish, a taxi service for the church and all its programs
- create, oversee, and often carry out the work of promotion and advertising
- carry a heavy part of the responsibility to collect sufficient income to run the church
- either run any new building program or be the chief expediter for seeing that it is completed

The conflict between this list and Paul's description of the job can be resolved by recognizing that although the pastor is in a real sense an administrator, there are four distinct areas of administration involved in running a church, not just one; and the pastor is directly responsible to administer only two of them. With this he can agree.

The diagram on the following page (figure 3) delineates the areas. The key to understanding this diagram is the phrase "primary source for responsibility." (The bylaws of the church will determine who carries the primary responsibility for administration of the congregation or corporation business.)

Now, as the administrative responsibilities of the pastor are separated from other administrative responsibilities, two things stand out: (1) the pastor does carry prime responsibility for certain areas of the church life, and (2) his responsibilities are, in fact, a contemporaneous description of the biblical office of the prophet, as understood in its etymological, not its sophisticated, New Testament use. The prophet (in Hebrew, "interpreter") is the one who explains or delivers the will of another. Therefore, in its root it does not carry the authority for inspiration or for miraculous acts or forecasting of events; the pastor is a prophet in the historic, generic use of the word.

The pastor, of course, cannot be totally divorced from any area of his church's life, even though he does not carry the prime

DIVISION OF ADMINISTRATIVE* RESPONSIBILITIES WITHIN A LOCAL CHURCH

BASIC AREAS OF RESPONSIBILITY TO BE ADMINISTERED	PASTOR: A "RESOURCE" AND A "SAFEGUARD" PERSON			
	PASTOR: Primary source for administration of:	PASTOR PLUS ELDERS: Primary source for administration of:	DEACONS: Primary source for administration of:	CONGREGATION/ (1) CORPORATION: Primary source for administration of:

	Preaching
	Teaching (2)
	Counseling
	Leadership (3)
		Worship
		Sacraments
		Membership
		Training and Orientation
		Care for the Flock (Example
		  Shepherding
		  Oversight
		  Guarding)
		Discipline
		Evangelism
		Missions
		Defense of the Faith
			Providing relief for financial needs (congregation and community)
			• Collecting gifts
			• Distributing
			• Teaching biblical lessons derived from such experience
			• Preventing poverty
			Acts of comfort and mercy to old, invalid, hospitalized, etc.
			Ministry to strengthen basic spiritual caliber of the congregation
				Election of Officers
				Calling the Pastor
				Determining the extent of denominational relationships
				Finances
				Building Programs
				Maintenance of building and grounds
				Social activities
				Community involvement

* In several instances, "administrative responsibility" is to be understood to include the responsibility actually to do the work involved.

(1) Often by delegation; e.g., finances to the Trustees of the Corporation.

(2) Particularly in preparation of Sunday School teachers, church officers, preparation of candidates for membership, etc.

(3) See discussion of leadership, chapter 4.

FIGURE 3

responsibility of its administration. The areas in which he clearly does not carry primary responsibility are the diaconal services of the church and the work of the congregation or corporation of the church. In these areas he serves, but as the resource person for the people. In order to do this he must, of course, be enough aware of the developments and problems in each of these areas to give occasional suggestions. He also serves as a safeguard person to raise warnings when methodology employed by the church is not God-honoring.[2]

The Office of the Ruling-Teaching Elder

This discussion of pastoral responsibility is based on a biblical warrant for the office of pastor as distinct from the office of ruling elder, or at least that within the framework of the office of ruling elder there is a special category for the office of pastor. More and more, sincere evangelical ministers and elders are questioning this presumption. Among rank and file membership of most churches there is no question and not even much discussion about whether the Bible distinguishes between teaching and ruling elders. Rather, most laymen are inclined to think there is almost something magical about the pastor's office; all too often they declare: "When we get a pastor who is a real leader, then the church will finally get off 'dead center,' and not before!" Inherent in such an attitude is the idea that the pastor has all the answers; that he can do everything that needs doing; that the office of pastor, when filled with the right man, is a special office unto itself; and that it is of the utmost importance. Unlike those who question the pastor's office, and unlike those who exalt it, I am persuaded that the office of pastor is a special category within the calling of the office of the ruling elder, giving him certain areas of responsibility that are specifically his, but making him equal, not superior, to the ruling elder in the responsibility of oversight.

Paul relates the offices of ruling elder and pastor-teacher by declaring that both are essentially ruling elders (1 Timothy 5:17), but that the pastor-teacher has a special calling, obligation, and privilege of service among his peers (that is, among the ruling elders). From this it is evident that there is, at least, a special category among the ruling elders for the special office of ruling-teaching elder. And this special office will demand special training,

---

2. See Part 4.

examination, and financing. It also demands an inherent necessity for special ability that will always include the ability to lead people.

Further insight into Paul's teaching about the office of the pastor-teacher comes out of his discussions on the gifts of the Spirit. He discusses these gifts to the members of the church in several passages: Romans 12:6-8; 1 Corinthians 12:4-10 and 28-30 (and on through chapters 13 and 14). Note that in Ephesians 4:11 Paul describes offices in the church into which God places specially gifted men rather than the specific gifts given to men. The first such office is that of apostle. The qualifications for this office are spelled out in Acts 1:21-22. From these verses it is clear that after the last apostle died no one else could ever meet the qualifications. Hence this office is closed.

Next is the office of prophet. We have already noted that when the word is used in its generic sense it is a good title for the work of the pastor-teacher. However, in its sophisticated New Testament sense it included the ability to make special revelations. Anyone today claiming such revelations would be adding to the Bible, and since the New Testament is now completed that activity cannot be accepted. Therefore, in its New Testament sense, the office of prophet also is closed.

This leaves the offices of evangelist and pastor-teacher. Actually, the New Testament evangelist was a church planter (e.g., Philip in Acts 8:4-12 and 21:8). This work is still going on. However, since it is related to "beginnings," not to the continuing work of a church, it is limited by its specialization. The remaining office, therefore, carries the great weight of responsibility to teach and to communicate the Bible to men and women. That office is filled by those designated in 1 Timothy 5:17 as the teaching elders. And the pastor-teacher is, in fact, a continuing gift even for the contemporary church, since God has not closed off its function.

Paul also states: "For the grace of God that brings salvation has appeared to all men. . . . These, then, are the things you should teach. Encourage and rebuke with all authority. Do not let any one despise you" (Titus 2:11, 15). It is evident from the tone of verse 15, especially in the light of verse 11, that Titus had a special task and the right relationship necessary to carry out that task.

In this light the meaning of Paul's instruction to Timothy about his ordination becomes an important argument: "Do not neglect your gift, which was given you through a prophetic message when the body of elders laid their hands on you. Be diligent in these matters; give yourself wholly to them, so that everyone may see your progress. Watch your life and doctrine closely. Persevere in them, because if you do, you will save both yourself and your hearers" (1 Timothy 4:14-16). "For this reason I remind you to fan into flame the gift of God, which is in you through the laying on of my hands" (2 Timothy 1:6). Paul tells Timothy that he had "a spiritual gift." Timothy clearly had many "gifts" of the Spirit, but Paul here refers to a special condition—a spiritual *gift* as the quality necessary to do the authoritative job, the leadership God called him to exercise. In a sense this gift parallels (possibly not point by point) the special anointing by God for Old Testament offices (Saul and David as kings, for example). Throughout history God has provided gifted men for leadership responsibility. This "gift" of Timothy's must have been his God-given ability of leadership resulting from the Holy Spirit's integrating and exciting the many individual gifts and graces resident in him. And therefore he was more accountable to God, not better than other Christians. This special accountability exists because of the special calling, obligation, and privilege of service placed upon the teaching elder among his peer ruling elders.

The Authority-Base for the Pastor-Teacher's Ministry

The pastor-teacher is always a ruling elder among ruling elders. True, his special calling to teach and preach (and its attendant special training, preparation, and examination) leads to his privilege of dealing with people on the basis of a pastoral relationship. However, the primary source for his authority in office is that he, with all the other ruling elders, is charged to give spiritual account for the souls of those to whom he ministers (Hebrews 13:17). The pastor, though never taking advantage of preparing and preaching a sermon to "pulpit whip" one person, nevertheless knows something of the needs of each of his people and must preach to meet them.

Failure to understand their authority-base is the major reason many young ministers leave their first pastorates for other professions. As students in seminary, they never considered that the authority upon which they should base their ministry is not the thoroughness of their education, nor their pulpit skill, nor even their native ability to communicate through a one-to-one counseling ministry. Actually most undergraduates have not even considered that their ministry of ruling elder means that *immediately*

38

upon ordination (which usually means *immediately* upon gradua-
tion) they must begin to rule over people and that people ultimately will respect or reject them on the basis of personal response to the minister's ruling. Therefore, it is not hard to see that
young ministers are in for almost insurmountable trouble when
they realize their responsibility to rule just at the moment they
begin practicing it. The ultimate implication is clear, however: the
office of ruling elder is the ground upon which the minister stands
as preacher-teacher to his people.

Certainly the pastor does not have this responsibility all by
himself—he is one among several ruling elders. But he does have a
unique base upon which to preach and teach and provide creative
leadership for his people.

The Pastor As a Unique Leader

In fact, the ability to provide leadership for his people is a key
qualification to function in this office. Both the biblically en-
joined responsibility to preach and teach (and to deal with the
consequences of these activities) and the daily experience of living
in the pastorate demand it. Indeed, it is impossible for him to
preach and to teach in anything but an ineffective way if he does
not lead the people through his preaching and teaching, through
his exemplary life, and through his harnessing to creative use the
various gifts that God has given to them. This is especially true
when they can be used to meet particular problems facing the
church or its sense of community.

The pastor-teacher is a gifted person given to the church by the
Holy Spirit (Ephesians 4:11) to build upon the evangelist's minis-
try. The gift (singular)—it bears repeating—must be the Holy
Spirit-given ability to integrate the many gifts (plural) and talents
given to him to provide a powerful creative force to motivate
God's people. That is leadership, pure and simple.

This leadership, which in the area of spiritual oversight coordi-
nates with that of the ruling elders, is vital to make the marvelous
Gospel of sovereign grace come alive to the people in their everyday lives and in the development of the entire church life. Consequently, it cannot be argued, as so many today try to do, that the
pastor had no special obligation to lead his people.

It is of interest to see the rather standard experience of
churches seeking to be distinctive, with great emphasis on their
organism as opposed to their organization, since these churches are

39

the most frequent expositors of the "no leadership by the pastor" concept. Figure 4 is presented on the basis of much personal experience, but admittedly without volumes of statistical data, since much of this material is highly subjective and cannot be reduced to objective statistics.

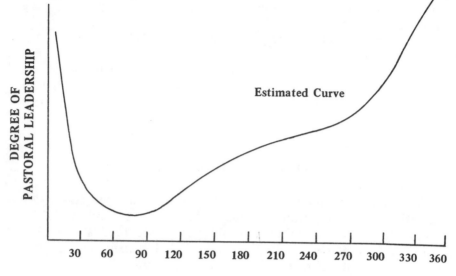

SUNDAY MORNING REGULAR ATTENDANCE
OF ORGANISM-ORIENTED CHURCHES

FIGURE 4

Three things are apparent from this chart:

1. When the group is *very* small, leadership is absolutely essential. Common agreement without trained leadership at this stage usually amounts only to a pooling of ignorance, regardless of the amount of sincerity involved. Indeed, another leader almost always emerges if the pastor doesn't provide leadership. This situation often produces the proverbial "two-headed monster" later on in the life of the church.

2. By the time the group is slightly larger, it has been forced by the need to stay involved or disintegrate (from lack of numbers) to share rapid growth in knowledge and a multitude of faith-stretching experiences. This sharing may suggest that, since everyone was mutually involved, the need for special leadership by the pastor probably is not necessary. And many may fear losing this precious blessing of "sharing" if pastoral leadership is exercised. Hence the degree of pastoral

40

leadership falls at this point, creating a frustrating experience for the pastor, who does not see how these sharing experiences could have happened in the first place were it not for his leadership.

3. When the group gets larger, sheer size and proportionately larger problems, plus the regular centralization of preaching and teaching by the pastor, make his leadership inevitable whether or not the congregation intends to have it.

One of the dangers implied above is the hesitancy with which the small, sharing group gives up that blessed intimacy of total involvement and rapid growth. Rather than give it up, some churches have decided to stay small. This is fine—if everyone can continue the experience of total involvement that was necessary just to keep alive during the beginning days. But most of the time, changing circumstances and a mobile society make that impossible. Also, the volume of time and energy involved to maintain a small church cannot be continued year after year by very many families. Therefore, even the small church would be wise to seek and recognize the blessing of a pastor's unique leadership.

Although biblical leadership by the pastor-teacher is limited to exclude any possibility of unilateral oversight of the congregation's spiritual growth and discipline, and is particularly limited in the areas in which the pastor is simply a safeguard or resource person, there is no limitation in providing creative leadership for the congregation through such things as:

- more meaningful worship
- unique ways of teaching
- evangelism
- application of the specific purpose for the church
- response to community needs
- specialized work with various age groups in the church
- missions involvement and empathy
- application of doctrinal truth to contemporary problems
- more ways to use the physical plant
- denomination or association involvement

Further, two facets of pastoral leadership must be understood and appreciated by the pastor, officers, and people alike:

1. The pastor often is in the best position to discern the gifts and talents of various members of the congregation. In this regard, his leadership is most fully demonstrated in:

41

- actively seeking such gifts and talents in every member of the church
- guiding the development of these gifts and talents even to the extent of personal teaching
- encouraging the individual to exercise these gifts and talents even to the extent of providing specific circumstances in which they can be used

2. The pastor many times is under great pressure to do almost everything himself, especially if he can do it so much better than anyone else. At those times his creativity in leadership is most fully demonstrated in not yielding to that pressure, but in demanding the opportunity for each "joint" to supply some blessing to the rest of the "body" (Ephesians 4:16).

Finally, and most importantly, the pastor's ministry and example of life is to be a leadership tool in the hand of the Holy Spirit to motivate the flock to continuous forward motion without losing the blessings of distinctive testimony or the blessings of being an organism. This forward motion crosses all aspects of Christianity. It includes the need continuously to present the Gospel of grace to the lost. Paul's personal example of commitment to this in 2 Timothy 2:10 and Romans 9:3 are testimonials that have kept men moving with the Gospel for generations. It includes the need for every Christian to continue to grow in grace. Paul's instruction to Titus and Timothy (Titus 2:2 ff.; 2 Timothy 2:24-26) describes the combination of example of life, gracious tact, positive action, and the need for the corporate church to continue to face and answer the contemporary challenges before it. Paul instructs Titus that he indeed has such a responsibility (Titus 3:1-2).

To sum up, the pastor's responsibility to be a leader means he is to be so subject to the person and work of the Holy Spirit that God uses him to keep the individual Christian and the corporate church from acting (volitionally or by presumption!) as if they "had already arrived!"

Conclusion

The pastor is the pastor-teacher, a ruling elder among peer ruling elders, charged in a special way with administering that part of the church's life that proclaims the Word of God and instructs unto discipleship. In its generic sense, the word "prophet" describes the pastor. He also serves his people with special effectiveness in additional areas as a resource person. No job can be more challenging than that of the pastor, especially since he must simultaneously serve both young and old, educated and noneducated, black and white, the spiritually mature and spiritual babies, and even some who are yet unborn the second time.

3
The Pastor: A Preacher
and a Teacher

The pastor exercises the major portion of his public ministry through preaching and teaching. In these ministries he is the prophet to his congregation (see chapter 2) by the authority rooted in the person of Jesus Christ as Prophet. As corollaries to this, his authority for providing the opportunity for complete worship and the incentive for total discipleship is rooted in the person of Jesus Christ as Priest, and his authority for handling the keys of the Kingdom to bind or loosen is rooted in the person of Jesus Christ as King.

Paul considers himself called as a prophet. He describes his calling by listing three distinct categories: "And of this gospel I was appointed a herald and an apostle and a teacher" (2 Timothy 1:11); "and for this purpose I was appointed a herald and an apostle—I am telling the truth, I am not lying—and a teacher of the true faith to the Gentiles" (1 Timothy 2:7). Since preacher, apostle, and teacher are listed in both passages, it is evident that Paul means the terms to be not synonymous but rather distinct one from the other. Note also that the immediate context of both of these verses is the magnitude of the Gospel. Paul's calling as preacher, apostle, and teacher, then, is surely rooted directly in the Gospel presentation. Paul relates this information to us about his calling as an apostle, thus authenticating it as the truth. He then, by declaring himself to be a preacher (taken from the Greek word for proclamation, *kērygma*), indicates he is under Holy Spirit injunction to proclaim this inspired truth. Finally, by declaring himself to be a teacher (taken from the Greek word for instruction, *didaskō*), he indicates he is under Holy Spirit injunction to instruct (by lesson and illustration) those who will hear this inspired truth. A meaningful deduction is now apparent from this study. Preaching is one specific ministry, and teaching is another specific ministry.

Preaching Ministry Defined

The preaching ministry will be considered first:

(a) Preaching is a proclamation of the Gospel to the unsaved: "But the Lord stood at my side and gave me strength, so that through me the message might be fully proclaimed and all the Gentiles might hear it. And I was delivered from the lion's mouth" (2 Timothy 4:17).

(b) Preaching is a proclamation of the whole counsel of God to the church: "Paul, a servant of God and an apostle of Jesus Christ for the faith of God's elect and the knowledge of the truth that leads to godliness—a faith and knowledge resting on the hope of eternal life, which God, who does not lie, promised before the beginning of time, and at his appointed season he brought his word to light through the preaching entrusted to me by the command of God our Savior" (Titus 1:1-3).

It is sad to see an increased downgrading of preaching in many circles today. In its place "discussion" is presented as "the" way for the church to be "with it," to be contemporary. There certainly is a place for discussions, but not as a substitute for preaching! It was not merely a cliché that Paul put bluntly to his readers in the church at Rome: "How, then, can they call on the one they have not believed in? And how can they believe in the one of whom they have not heard? And how can they hear without someone preaching to them?" (Romans 10:14).

A secondary conclusion must be drawn from the discussion thus far: the ministry of preaching *will always* be part of the life and work of the church!

Ineffectual Preaching

Having established the validity and continuity of the preaching ministry, the question occurs, "Why is preaching apparently so ineffectual?" But before answering that question, certain travesties parading under the guise of preaching should be exposed and labeled for what they are. One is the practice of ranting on and on from the pulpit with what amounts to nothing more than an emotional harangue. This is often called preaching, but it is really nothing more than a discharge of emotional verbiage designed to motivate the hearers, usually to an emotional action. It is not a proclamation of authoritative truth, which seeks to challenge the whole person to a response.

Another travesty is the low-key interlacing of Bible verses with no regard to their context or to proper laws of hermeneutics. Such "preaching" often leaves the listener with a feeling of awe at the knowledge of the preacher, but with no increase of his own comprehension of the Bible itself, and is not to be confused with valid Bible commentary preaching.

"Preaching" of these kinds usually has an ulterior motive, or at least a false consequence. It seems best designed to prove some new "truth" or to legitimize some rash action of an individual or institution. Also, this kind of "preaching" usually leaves the "preacher" free of responsibility when the listener tries to apply what he has heard to his life.

Effectual Preaching

Yet even preaching that is free from these errors may be fruitless, although no one could say that of Peter's and Paul's preaching. Analyzing their sermons reveals at least one major truth about apostolic preaching: the listeners clearly felt personally involved in what was preached! The apostles proclaimed the Gospel and the whole counsel of God in terms relating the listener to the Lord in the context of the listener's everyday needs and experiences.

Applying this standard to today's evangelical preaching soon reveals a failure to communicate this involvement. This has been happening for so long that many church members don't know what it is that is missing in preaching, although they often realize instinctively that something is radically wrong. And when they grope for an explanation of the lack of power in the preaching, they find only superficial causes. For instance, they say, the preacher

- has no enthusiasm when he preaches; or
- has too much enthusiasm for such a solemn occasion
- has a "squeaky" voice that rasps one's nerves; or
- has such a soft voice and singsong manner that it puts the listener to sleep
- doesn't have any "meat" in his sermons, just many little, inconsequential illustrations; or
- doesn't use any illustrations and its just "too heavy" for the average layman

The very fact that many of these criticisms are contradictions of each other indicates that the listeners are too involved with the techniques of the preacher and not involved enough with the relationship of the message to their everyday needs and experiences. Techniques have a place of importance, and every preacher must learn to be the most effectual preacher he can. Yet it should be plain by now that good preaching, though enhanced by the preacher's developing his natural talents into powerful techniques, is measured by how well it relates the listener to life. Think of men who have preached to congregations with such success that God, as a direct consequence of their preaching, continuously blesses their ministry through lives being changed for the glory of God. With no difficulty, several eminently successful preachers could be identified who, among them, had all these faults and yet God used them. One such minister (well known by me) sounds like a man speaking with a mouthful of gravel; he never preaches less than forty-five minutes, his vocabulary is phenomenal in scope and always used to the greatest possible extent, and he often doesn't muster enough pulpit exuberance apparently to excite anyone; but the fact remains that God is mightily blessing his preaching ministry. Through his sermons his listeners are invariably drawn closer to the Lord in their everyday experiences.

Preaching—the way Peter and Paul did it—successfully makes the Bible become *God revealing himself as the living God and demonstrating that he continues to work in his creation today.* In other words, preaching leads to worship.

Effectual Preaching Developed

Certainly the minister must have thorough training in homiletics, hermeneutics, apologetics, systematic theology, and the like, so that he may develop and skillfully deliver worthwhile content from the Word of God. But this is the beginning, not the end, of his preparation. That training does nothing to provide the insight necessary to make possible the listener's involvement; the insight must exist as an inherent facet of the gift of ministering (see chapter 2). However, assuming it is present, it can be strengthened and developed, and careful, long-range sermon preparation is the tool to help do it. Such preparation demands a high degree of personal discipline, but the dividends it provides are surely worth the cost. One such method of sermon preparation is spelled out below to exemplify this concept.

1. During the summer, plan in general outline form sermons for the next twelve months. At that time choose the Bible sections to preach from for the next year, determine the overall controlling theme of each section, and determine the more specific expressions of those themes. (An alternate time frame would be to plan the preaching either in quarters or according to traditional church year divisions; at least six, preferably nine months ahead, choose sections and determine themes as outlined above. This would mean a quarterly planning session of material six to nine months ahead.)

2. Two months ahead of the scheduled time to preach, study the Scripture itself in sufficient depth to develop an outline of the theme and the prime subordinate parts of each division of the outline. Consequently, each week some preparation will be necessary for a sermon to be preached two months later.

3. During the next two months, make notes of any experiences, reading, and conversations that seem to relate to the theme of the sermon. The point here is that once one is alert to a given theme, its application will become evident in all kinds of circumstances in which it would otherwise go unnoticed.

4. For at least one-third of the sermons, discuss the theme and the proposed development of it with an elder or with any member or friend in the congregation at least a week before the sermon is delivered. Carefully note ideas, reactions, and suggestions to add to the store of related material gathered over the previous two months. This will provide several things:

   (a) a source of "down-to-earth" wisdom;
   (b) a sounding board to assess before preaching how successfully the form communicates the content;
   (c) for the church member, the joy of knowing he has made a meaningful contribution to the pastor and, through him, to the church;
   (d) a means to stop "preacher criticism" throughout the congregation before it starts.

5. During the last week of preparation, think through the accumulated data and develop from them a few statements that describe how their basic theme relates to life. Then carefully assess the conclusions to be sure they conform to biblical doctrine. If they do, then filter the sermon preparation through these findings. It will make the Bible come alive for

preacher and listeners alike. Finally, work into the sermon specific illustrations where possible.

6. Before actually delivering the sermon, test the entire message, in its respective parts and as a whole, against the possible kinds of reception one could expect by various people in the congregation. Play "devil's advocate" against the sermon to be sure it stands the test of communication.

7. Throughout this entire process, and particularly just before preaching, be spiritually sensitive to the great issues involved in the sermon, as well as the small details, and be willing to be committed to the conclusions drawn from the sermon at any cost. Weigh carefully the price involved in making this a "life sermon" *for* the pastor rather than merely an "academic sermon" *from* the pastor, and only preach it if it is a "life sermon."

8. Finally, be sure that the sermon is indeed a proclamation—thus says the Lord—and directed to the listener! In a real sense, preach so that every sermon will force men to live through a confrontation with God.

This kind of effort will keep the preparation from being little more than an academic exercise in the antiseptic atmosphere of the study and the sermon from being little more than an academically and doctrinally perfect essay to which is mechanically added a "real-life" story every so often to make it "alive."

Teaching Ministry Defined

Teaching, too, is a specific ministry—a ministry given by God to instruct the Christian in his faith and its practice; it leads to discipleship. In Ephesians 4:11 Paul lists the offices graciously given by God to the church, concluding with the continuing offices of evangelist (actually the church-planter) and pastor-teacher. The pastor-teacher is, of course, also a ruling elder (see 1 Timothy 5:17-18), which means he teaches (as well as preaches) from the authority of the ruling elder/pastor. The minister teaches the written Word of God, which is inspired as originally given, without error and infallible, to Christians who "have put on the new self, which is being renewed in knowledge in the image of its Creator" (Colossians 3:10). His special mission is to teach in the light of the understanding of his flock gained from ruling over them; his goal is to enable them to become true disciples of Christ. This definition is further substantiated by the Great Commission itself, in which Jesus instructs his church to "make disciples" (*mathēteuō*).

Discipleship Defined

The minister, consequently, must have a deep understanding of his goal of discipleship if he is to carry it out. Discipleship has been defined many times. One minister, the Reverend Paul Alexander, pastor of the Reformed Presbyterian Church in Huntsville, Alabama, has formulated a practical definition on which he has developed a ministry that God has abundantly blessed. His definition will be used as a foundation for the discussion of the pastor-teacher's teaching ministry:

> Christian Disciple: One whose life is integrated around the worship of Christ.

Mr. Alexander comments on his definition:

> I like to emphasize the relationship between the word "disciple" and the word "discipline." *A disciple is one who comes under the discipline of another.* A Christian comes under the discipline of Jesus Christ as Lord and Savior. At the outset, a disciple may be a follower from afar who comes under the discipline of Christ only to the extent that a mild curiosity or passing fancy regarding Christ might hold him: As this disciple matures (the Holy Spirit effectually calls him), the disciple is captivated heart, soul, mind, and strength (Matthew 22:37) by the God-Man. From being mildly curious, he becomes the awed worshiper of Christ. The expression of Thomas in John 20:28, "My Lord and my God," reflects this process brought to fruition.

Mr. Alexander further points out that

> man is a worshiping creature by definition, that all his life is ruled by worship, and he does not have a choice as to whether he will worship or not—his only choice is what he will worship. The Christian evangelist calls men from the worship of a thousand false gods to the worship of the true God, and this worship pervades all of life, serving as the spiritual foundation for all personal relationships and human endeavors.

The Basic Facets of the Teaching Ministry

One key in Mr. Alexander's definition is the sentence, "A disciple is one who comes under the discipline of another." When this point is related to the direct call for worship in his definition of discipleship, three basic facets of the teaching ministry of the pastor-teacher take focus.

1. His teaching always has a specific goal, and that is to enable his flock to glorify and enjoy God through discipleship.
2. His teaching will always be goal-oriented in its presentation. It must supply his flock with the knowledge they need to accomplish the goal. Also, it must supply them with all the incentives given in the Bible for the application of this knowledge to life. Finally, it must allow for each individual to be fed according to his own needs so that each will grow in grace from his present degree of maturity.
3. The goal and orientation of his teaching determine the basic, minimum truths that he must be sure his people know in order to be responsible disciples. These truths are:

   - what God is
   - what man is
   - what keeps man and God apart
   - how man is reconciled to God
   - where man learns about God
   - why man can believe the Bible
   - what God expects of man
   - what God accepts as worship

The Minister Is the Pastor-Teacher

Central to this discussion, of course, is the fact that the authoritative ministry of pastor-teacher must be reserved for the minister, regardless of the gifts of teaching with which other individuals in the church are blessed. To help make this distinction clear between the pastor-teacher and other teachers in the church, the latter could be called teacher-teachers. The teacher-teacher labors in one of three major areas:

1. In the supporting work of church member, as a Sunday School teacher, Bible class teacher, and the like. These people are often specially gifted and blend marvelously into

51

the total ministry of the church for the glory of God. Still, it is necessary to distinguish between them and the pastor-teacher in order to emphasize the responsibility placed on the latter as pastor, ruling elder, and teacher of that particular flock. When this distinction is lost in a church, all too often factions surface and soon split the church (see 1 Corinthians 1 ff.).

2. In the secular teaching profession. Most of the time these people are deeply dedicated to the training of students, finding fulfillment themselves in the task of shaping lives. They supplement this fulfillment (and rightly so) with the professional pride of a professional job well done. In the church, they can be the cause of one major pastoral frustration just because they know so well how to teach. The pastor teaches from an authority base reserved only for the elders. He usually has been well trained in content, but he seldom has had any pedagogy. Unless he is a "natural" teacher, his ability to teach what he knows is usually limited. When the congregation, or, even worse, the pastor himself, begins to compare pastor techniques in teaching with teacher-teacher techniques, the pastor often wants to quit! If he truly is called, of course, he cannot give up. Instead he should work to develop the technique of teaching—even get some pointers from one of those super-teachers.

3. In blind commitment to a philosophy or cause, seeking to win converts to his "god." Most of the time these teachers espouse anti-Christian positions. Occasionally a sincere but misguided Christian falls into this category by trying to replace the Holy Spirit's work of calling people to Christ by his own salesmanship. Even pastor-teachers can fall into this kind of teaching practice rather than depend on the Holy Spirit. When this happens, the minister often begins to emphasize some minor (or heretical) point as if it is the whole essence of the Gospel, thus distorting and even destroying his ministry.

There is danger in equating the gift of pastor-teacher with that of teacher-teacher. A godly man, gifted as a teacher-teacher, whose calling is to increase the mental resources of his students so that the whole student is trained, cannot presume that he also is called to be a pastor simply because he is both a Christian and a good teacher. He is a teacher-teacher, not a pastor-teacher. Too often sincere men have falsely assumed that this combination automatically constitutes a call by the Holy Spirit and have gone into the ministry only to bring themselves and their families into deep anguish and trial, occasionally feeling themselves to be total failures in life. Only when the pastor-teacher appreciates the ground of authority for his teaching and the purpose of his teaching will he begin to understand what his teaching is all about. He will be teaching in the biblical way: teaching the written Word of God, in the light of the understanding he has gained of his flock from ruling over them, in order to enable them to become true disciples of Christ.

The Pastor-Teacher Is
the Authority Consultant for Discussions

Further contrast between the two teachers appears in discussion groups. The exclusive use of such groups to communicate successfully to contemporary man has already been ruled out. However, in discussion groups dealing with the basics of faith and life, a teacher-teacher may be qualified as the immediate source of needed data but not for serving as the authority consultant. The pastor-teacher is needed as the authority consultant since errors will probably occur and have to be corrected on the spot, and priorities relative to the material under discussion will have to be discerned and declared.

Maximizing His Teaching Ministry

The teaching pastor must avoid three common errors. He must not be guilty of substituting a random "potpourri" of comments on current events for true pastor-teacher teaching; he must not be guilty of merely substituting a massive amount of Bible data for true pastor-teacher teaching; and finally, he must not be guilty of not teaching at all, a failure often based on the false premise that he is called to preach and can't do both, especially on the same day—Sunday.

One effective way to maximize his teaching ministry is through Sunday School teaching. I believe that the minister should arrange to teach different age groups of the church throughout the year, with a special emphasis on the teenagers. He might do well to refuse to be the perennial "adult class" teacher. One way to accomplish this is to teach an introductory course from January through April to candidates for church membership, then teach all the high school young people for four or five weeks. The minister can take this opportunity to teach material that demands his specialized training (such as the doctrine of inspiration and canonicity) or the prestige of his office (such as the blessings and the dangers of social practices, especially between the sexes).

Following this teaching, the minister could teach the junior high young people, even using the same material but gearing it down to their level. In every class the teacher would have the option of attending his own or the adult class. Then during the summer months the pastor could teach the adult class and fill in for any Sunday School class whose teacher is on vacation. In the fall he could teach the adult class for four weeks, again teach the high school, junior high school, and grade school classes, and finally take a block of weeks before the end of the year to be on call if needed, but not to teach any particular class.

One of the greatest blessings a minister can enjoy lies in discerning between his preaching and teaching ministries, accomplishing the biblical objective for each, and using them not only to supplement each other but also to complement each other. The minister surely must be preacher and teacher!

4

The Pastor: The Deacon
of His Congregation

While addressing a seminary class on how to prepare sermons, an elderly man of God, Dr. L. L. Lathem of Chester, Pennsylvania, was asked by a young seminarian, "If I'm to prepare two sermons each Sunday, a Sunday School lesson and a midweek Bible study, where will I get all the material I need about which to preach?" Without any hesitation, the old warrior-saint answered, "That's easy, son. Just get to know two books inside and out and you will never lack for material. The two books are the Bible and your church's roll book!"

The illustration introduces the fact that a minister is to know his people so that he can serve their needs. The apostle Paul shows the validity of this knowledge when he points out that he was made a *minister* so that he might *fully* carry out the preaching of the Word of God (Colossians 1:23, 25). This word "minister" ("servant") translates the Greek word *diakonos* ("deacon"). It could be said that Paul was declaring that he had to become a deacon in order to preach effectively.

Serving: Necessary Prerequisite to Preaching

Paul was simply echoing our Lord. Jesus said of himself that "the Son of Man did not come to be served, but to serve, and to give his life a ransom for many" (Matthew 20:28), thus declaring that he himself was to be a deacon as it were, since the word "serve" is another translation of *diakonos.* Paul is so committed to this facet of ministry that he applies it as a title to Jesus: "For I tell you that Christ has become a servant of the Jews on behalf of God's truth, to confirm the promises made to the patriarchs . . . " (Romans 15:8).

The idea of serving-ministering—acting in the frame of reference of the deacon—was very well known to the early church. In verb form alone the *diakonos* root occurs more than thirty times in the New Testament. In all its forms, it is translated as deacon, administer, minister, serve, administration, ministration, ministry, office, and the like. Paul applies it directly to himself and to Tychicus in Ephesians 3:7 and 6:21.

The evidence is plain that Jesus, Paul, the disciples, and the early church were deeply involved in the concept of ministering to one another. Surely it is self-evident that the pastor—the undershepherd of the flock—must emulate Jesus, the Great Shepherd, and have a ministry of serving. In a real sense the pastor is a deacon—a pastor-deacon. Without this facet of ministry his service as a ruling elder could become a hierarchical dictatorship and his service as a preacher and teacher would soon become exercises in academics.

An Attitude of Heart Is Necessary

How does the pastor develop this ministry? Certainly not simply by wishing for it to come naturally. There must be a special attitude of heart motivating him in all circumstances and special activities of ministry to express this attitude to the fullest.

A Heart Committed to Serve

Before getting into those activities, some presuppositions should be declared. The first is that, based on material in the Gospels, the life of Christ is understood only when the ministry of serving is appreciated as one of its major thrusts. And any minister intending to glorify Christ will regularly check for this thrust in his own daily life and acts of devotion and consecration to the Lord.

A Heart of Humility

The second presupposition is that two characteristics must constantly operate as guiding forces in the pastor-deacon's heart. One is a powerful awareness of the spirit of humility. The apostle Paul uses the Lord Jesus as the ultimate demonstration of this: "Do nothing out of selfish ambition or vain conceit, but in humility consider others better than yourselves. Your attitude should be the same as that of Christ Jesus: Who, being in very nature God, did not consider equality with God something to be grasped, but made himself nothing, taking the very nature of a servant, being made in human likeness. And being found in appearance as a man, he humbled himself and became obedient to death—even death on a cross" (Philippians 2:3, 5-8). This spirit of humility puts the pastor-deacon's own estimation of himself in proper perspective to his estimation of those around him.

A Heart of Concern:
No Individual Is Unimportant

The other characteristic is a concern for people. Jesus felt this concern: "Jesus went through all the towns and villages, teaching in their synagogues, preaching the good news of the kingdom and healing every kind of disease and sickness. When he saw the crowds, he had compassion on them, because they were harassed and helpless, like sheep without a shepherd. Then he said to his disciples, 'The harvest is plentiful but the workers are few. Ask the Lord of the harvest, therefore, to send out workers into his harvest field' " (Matthew 9:35-38). Today it is easy for a minister to lose his awareness that everyone in the mass of humanity around him is actually a person who was created in God's own image with personal, individual identity. Or he might find himself thinking of the multitude as merely a vast diamond mine in which are hidden a few precious gems for him to unearth along with tons of valueless rock and dirt. Jesus never entertained such a base concept of the multitude he saw! His heart saw each one as an individual made in the image of God, a sheep without a shepherd!

For further evidence that Jesus saw men and women as individuals of worth, study the "I am" passages of the Gospel of John. Here are several:

> Then Jesus declared, "I am the bread of life. He who comes to me will never go hungry, and he who believes in me will never be thirsty" (John 6:35).

> When Jesus spoke again to the people, he said, "I am the light of the world. Whoever follows me will never walk in darkness, but will have the light of life" (John 8:12).

> Therefore Jesus said again, "I tell you the truth, I am the gate for the sheep. All who ever came before me were thieves and robbers, but the sheep did not listen to them" (John 10:7-8).

57

Jesus said to her, "I am the resurrection and the life. He who believes in me will live, even if he dies; and whoever lives and believes in me will never die. Do you believe this?" (John 11:25-26).

Again, Jesus' action illustrates this point. While he was in the district of Tyre and Sidon, a Canaanite woman cried out for mercy, especially for the healing of her daughter. The disciples wanted nothing to do with her; in fact, they seemed annoyed or embarrassed by her, or both. As a Canaanite and a woman, she had no right to detain them, and they wanted her sent away. But Jesus had concern for her and took the time to probe her heart with piercing questions. Finally, he responded to her and said, " 'Woman, you have great faith! Your request is granted.' And her daughter was healed from that very hour" (Matthew 15:28).

On other occasions his dealing in love with tiny children; with a Samaritan woman in the heat of the day; and, even in the depths of his own agony, with a thief and murderer, all demonstrate that no one was so unimportant to Jesus that he would not minister to him.

Today's minister must see people as Christ saw them. Only as this kind of humility and concern becomes the natural attitude of a minister's heart will he ever become a pastor-deacon. One of Satan's most powerful tools is to tempt a minister not to see all people as having worth, or else tempt him to give up on a person after repeated attempts to help. Several years ago a radio broadcast dramatized this temptation by relating an incident in the history of the Pacific Garden Mission in Chicago. One individual, constantly drunk, never ceased to disrupt the services of the rescue mission. Eventually the staff wanted to keep him out of the meetings. The director said, "No! He may come in if he wants to." Shortly before his death, the drunkard came to Jesus. In the last months of his life he was transformed into a walking witness to Christ's grace and power, and one person after another responded by accepting Christ. How wonderful, from the point of view of human responsibility and concern for the worth of a man, that the mission director believed that even that drunkard was important!

A Consequence:
Never Be Too Busy for People

A corollary to this conviction involves the attitude that it is necessary to minister unto, rather than to be ministered to. Putting it colloquially this corollary is: *If you're too busy to take time for individual people and their needs, you're too busy!* Jesus, when passing through Jericho, was surrounded by a crowd of people eagerly listening to everything he said—some in search of blessing to their souls, others in search of something that might eventually be used against him. In the midst of all that Jesus took time to stop the crowd, still it so that he could be heard at some distance, and look up into a tree and summon a little man with a questionable reputation to come down and fellowship with him personally. Again, while hanging on the cross, Jesus took time to appreciate the new earthly needs his mother was about to face, and he commended her into John's care. Today's minister can become so involved with "big" things that he feels it is a nuisance to have to take time to fellowship with a "little" man who isn't part of the crowd firing "deep" and "penetrating" questions at him. However, unless his heart is humbled and "little" people are as important as "big" issues, that minister does not have the foundation to be a servant as was Jesus.

Areas of Service

With the heart's attitude established, the discussion can now go on to the special activities that express the ministry of serving to the fullest. Again, the pattern will be the life of our Lord.

The pastor-deacon must develop an appreciation of people from the point of view that they have needs that must be met and that it is a high calling to serve them by attempting to meet their needs. In some cases the needs will be primarily physical, in others spiritual. In all cases there are sure to be spiritual connotations, and the pastor-deacon must always wrestle with the deeper needs as well as with the apparent needs. And he might as well realize that many people do not want their needs to be known, or do not really know that they have needs, or, if they know they have needs, do not understand themselves well enough to appreciate just what their needs really are. The pastor-deacon dare not be dissuaded from attempting to serve these people until he is openly rebuffed.

The matter of meeting these needs could be considered from one of two points of view: the needs themselves of the average congregation or the pastor's perspective as he ministers to his people. The latter will serve best here because of its ready parallels to the person and work of Jesus himself.

59

(a) *The responsibility to alleviate the physical needs of the sheep.* Frequently throughout his active ministry, Jesus healed the sick. On occasion he fed multitudes. He even made wine for a wedding feast. In short, he was sensitive to physical needs, to pain and sickness, and met them even when his associates felt he needed to stop and rest. Now, of course, deacons are involved in service to the destitute or ill, and more about their work will come later in this book. The pastor-deacon should be so aware of his flock that he spots most of these needs himself, and his deacons should fill him in on all the rest of them. However, in addition to this, he should have a telephone network set up for funneling information to him when accidents occur, or when people are hospitalized for any reason. Each circumstance must be ministered to as a new opportunity to share the love of Christ and point to the comfort and strength only given by the Holy Spirit himself.

(b) *The need to motivate sheep to live lives of service.* The minister must excite his people to concerned service of others. To do this he must understand what motivated Jesus to serve. The great motivating force in the work of Jesus was, of course, love, and that force was never more evident than in his washing the disciples' feet. Like Jesus, the pastor-deacon must be willing to do anything necessary to make the sheep aware that the greatness of God's kingdom is service in love. By washing the disciples' feet, Jesus showed the necessity for constant cleansing of the Christian's life as their daily consecration to service in love. From this point it is not difficult to see the magnitude of the Lord's teaching about such a small thing as a cup of cold water: "For I was hungry and you gave me something to eat, I was thirsty and you gave me something to drink, I was a stranger and you invited me in" (Matthew 25:35). Again, from the vantage point of service in love, the power of the Beatitudes rings clear (Luke 11:41). Even the true meaning of the so-called golden rule validates the concept of service in love (see Luke 6:27, 36). The pastor-deacon must be the living example that to serve in love *also* means receiving service given in love. This surely is one of the great voids of today's Christianity!

(c) *The need to rescue lost sheep.* An entirely different need always facing the pastor-deacon is rescuing the lost sheep.

60

Here again Christ was motivated by love, not by fear of losing numbers or of losing face before the world. In Luke 15 the parable of the lost sheep and the lost coin demonstrate that the individual is so important to Christ that he will go anywhere to reach one. Today's pastor-deacon, in order to rescue just one straying sheep, may have to go to equally strange places indeed, spend nights in pleading and prayer, wonder time and again if that person really is worthwhile in the long run. From the human point of view, the lost must see that we love them if they are to see that God loves them. Otherwise they are just "scalps" for the belt of the numbers-oriented "preacher." Therefore, the pastor-deacon is often the best evangelist there is. A marvelous picture of this eternal rescue service can be drawn from the beginning and the end of Christ's earthly ministry. At its beginning John the Baptist looked at Christ and declared that he was the Lamb of God. During his death, Jesus cried out "Father, forgive them, for they do not know what they are doing." Even after that, he had time to listen to the soul of the repentant thief and promise that he would join him that day in paradise! He served from beginning to end in order to rescue the lost. John put it all together: "This is love, not that we loved God, but that he loved us and sent his Son as an atoning sacrifice for our sins" (1 John 4:10).

(d) *The need to preserve the sheep of his flock.* The pastor-deacon must be committed to serve the least of the lambs, to protect and feed him. Again and again love is the great mover for both pastor and people. See it in Jesus, who prayed for Peter: "But I have prayed for you, Simon, that your faith may not fail. And when you have returned to me, strengthen your brothers" (Luke 22:32). Later that night "the Lord turned and looked straight at Peter. Then Peter remembered the word the Lord had spoken to him: 'Before the rooster crows today, you will disown me three times.' And he went outside and wept bitterly" (Luke 22:61-62). Peter saw such love and agony in the face of Jesus that he gave himself up to the hostile crowd, in spite of his earlier renunciation and profanity. Jesus had responded to the need of Peter. Hebrews 7:25 declares that, in fact, Jesus is constantly interceding for the preservation of every one of his sheep: "Therefore he is able to save completely those who come to God through him, because he always lives to intercede for them." This must take *some*

61

doing on Christ's part! For the pastor-deacon in everyday life this means developing his pulpit and pastoral ministry to encourage all his flock to be concerned in a like-minded way for each other, especially to be willing to forgive one another. Luke 17:3-4 describes true forgiveness: "So watch yourselves. If your brother sins, rebuke him, and if he repents, forgive him. If he sins against you seven times in a day, and seven times returns to you and says 'I repent,' forgive him." Matthew 18:35 reinforces it: "This is how my heavenly Father will treat each of you unless you forgive your brother from your heart." The pastor-deacon, by serving his flock in preaching, teaching, and demonstrating concern for each sheep to be preserved, is emulating the servant of God. As the pastor-deacon serves to bring about soul healing among his flock, he is achieving tremendous strides in the preservation of each Christian involved.

(e) *The need to counsel, encourage, and comfort the sheep of the flock.* Another way of serving one's people is beautifully demonstrated in John 20:16. Mary Magdalene had been to the tomb and told Peter and the others that it was empty. Peter and John also went and then had gone home. Mary came back. While weeping, she first saw two angels and then saw Jesus, but thought he was the gardener. Jesus spoke to her: "Mary!" (v. 16) and then said: "Do not hold on to me, for I have not yet returned to the Father. Go instead to my brothers and tell them, 'I am returning to my Father and your Father, to my God and your God' " (v. 17). He counseled her ("Do not hold on to me") so that she could put things into perspective, and then he encouraged her by instructing her exactly what to do.

The pastor-deacon must be at this ministry constantly. It is important to see that Jesus did not just counsel his disciples to pray by only giving to them some general guidance about prayer. He took time to instruct them personally in detail how to pray—"This is how you should pray . . . " (Matthew 6:9a). Today's minister dare not take it for granted that his people know how to pray, either. For that matter, the minister must remember that the new convert does not really know how to read his Bible or conduct personal devotions. In each of these cases the pastor-deacon will serve them by taking the time to counsel by instruction and example.

Much debate goes on about the proper philosophic foundation upon which to conduct a counseling ministry. Regardless of the position chosen, no minister can ignore the lessons from the life of Jesus. Even when with personal friends, Jesus did not hesitate to counsel, and he did it with grace, wisdom, and *specific direction* (as opposed to those who want the counselor never to express any opinion). For instance, when Martha was distracted by the many physical preparations involved in being hostess, Jesus said to her, "Martha, Martha . . . you are worried and upset about many things, but only one thing is needed. Mary has chosen what is better, and it will not be taken away from her" (Luke 10:41-42).

(f) *The need to pray for himself.* Probably the greatest need the pastor-deacon must meet is his own; his readiness to serve requires personal dependence by him and his wife on the love of God, since it often means humility, loneliness, and great sacrifice. As the pastor-deacon he will not only have the privilege of participating in his flock's experiences of greatest joy, but he will also have the responsibility of going through deepest shock and profoundest sorrow with them. His presence in both joy and sorrow will be the cement (the preaching and teaching, of course, being the building blocks) that makes the "pastoral relationship" a fulfilling experience. But being "cement" is almost always a traumatic experience for the minister. He will not be ready for it if he has not prepared himself day by day to be dependent on God for wisdom, graciousness, strength, and everything else necessary. When talented preachers fail in the pastorate, the number one reason is that they have not recognized their own need, have not paid the price of becoming ready to serve, and consequently have been bypassed by God as his instrument for service at the moment of need in someone's life. Jesus, upon the death of John the Baptist, "withdrew by boat privately to a solitary place" (Matthew 14:13). He was confronted by a multitude; he healed the sick, taught them, and then fed them with five loaves and two fish. Then, immediately thereafter, he sent the multitudes away and went to a mountain to pray by himself (Matthew 14:23). If Jesus himself needed internal renewal as he faced the trauma of service in his ministry, how much more do mere mortals need the same refreshment from God!

In the Garden of Gethsemane, apart from even his intimate three, Jesus won our salvation. He, as a man, completely surrendered to the will of God. It was through that blood-and-sweat prayer experience that he prepared himself to pay for our salvation on the cross of Calvary. And on the cross he was the supreme deacon—the suffering servant—the man of sorrows serving the will of his heavenly Father.

From Jesus himself, then, the message to the minister is loud and clear. The pastor-deacon must first be ready with God and renewed before God, day by day, if he is to serve his people. Then—he is to serve indeed!

5

A Potpourri
on Being a Minister

This chapter will offer old-fashioned advice.

The life of the minister has many more facets than the major ones dealt with so far. Most of the minor activities are minor because they are related to specific biblical requirements only generally and because they are the stuff of everyday life, not the dramatic or glamorous experiences of crisis decisions. Yet they are often the very things that ultimately make or break a ministry.

The material in this chapter is a reflection of years of experience (both in the pastorate itself and as a consultant to many other pastors), given as advice. No extensive effort will be made to relate the material to specific Bible verses; it all comes by practical extension and application from such verses as Matthew 6:33 and Romans 12:1-2.

Because of the nature of this material, its presentation will be topical, with each topic developed only enough to illustrate the point involved.

How to Live with Family Responsibilities

Family Involvement in the Ministry—Wife and Children

"How much should my entire family be involved with me in my call and my particular ministry?" This question is asked by most ministers sometime during their ministry, or it should be.

The answer involves many subjects, especially the place of the minister's wife in her role as the wife of the pastor and mother of their children. The subject could fill another book.

Several key points must be made, however. In the first place, the minister's wife has not been "called" (see chapter 2) in the same sense as her husband. However, our God is not a God of division and confusion. He will not "lead" the husband one way and the wife in the opposite way. Therefore, the minister's wife must daily seek the fullness of biblical subjection to her husband and the blessing of the fruit of the Spirit growing in her own life in tune with her husband's calling, so that she begins to share the burden of her husband's calling. Coupled with those dedications, she must take every opportunity to appreciate and understand his work and the message he preaches, so that she always can empathize and occasionally even sympathize with him and can co-labor whenever the situation permits. These activities, thus joined, will indeed bring her to share in his calling.

Next, she should make an unwavering commitment never to develop a totally other or additional pastoral relationship with the congregation. If she does allow herself to become a kind of "co-pastor," she will, in effect, be constructing a "two-headed monster" to lead the church, regardless of how sincere she is.

Another unwavering commitment she must make is to be first of all her husband's wife and mother of their children. To be sure, this commitment will affect the extent of her activity in the church and community and will influence her involvement with other people.

Lest these comments seem hard, it must be pointed out that they are presented in the context of beginning to share her husband's calling and continuing to grow in that sharing. This means that in each case the particular application of these concepts will lead her to conclusions that are her own, will probably differ under different circumstances and at different periods of her life, and will be her means of living in peace with her God.

It goes almost without saying, however, that these conclusions, properly understood, completely rule out the idea that to be a minister's wife is to have a "role" to play. The minister's wife is not one person in public and a different person in the privacy of her own home. She must always be herself. The congregation must consider it part of their responsibility to enable and encourage her always to be herself.

One of the practical ways the minister can help both his wife and his children live with his calling is to consider them participants in his call too (see Ephesians 5). Then they, too, will share his sense of calling, his victories for Christ, and his defeats. Such a little thing as praying about "our family's calling" instead of "my calling" during family devotions helps to develop just such an involvement as this.

Another practical thing he can do is to set apart some time to spend with his wife and children each day. During this time, un-hurried devotions and interpersonal relationships should be the order of the day. Remember, in spite of the slogans used to pro-mote little league ball clubs and the like, in the long run it is the quality and usefulness of the time a father spends with his children that does the most to shape their lives, not the quantity of time spent with them. However, such a use of his time demands of the minister a willingness both to arrange the time necessary and to make decisions based on priorities, recognizing therein that some things are too low on the totem pole of priorities and never will get done. (See chapter 10 for a discussion on priorities and goal setting.)

Furthermore, both the minister and his wife should accept the fact that their children will be brought up in a special kind of atmosphere. Rather than being a burden for the children to bear, it is actually a marvelous blessing for the children to enjoy. Obvi-ously they cannot be exposed to all the details of the struggles and trials of the church families going through battles with temptation and sin. But, as the children of the manse, they are privileged to have the direct work of God in the midst of his people ebb and flow about them day by day, often right there in their own home. If the minister and his wife properly supervise this natural involve-ment, their children will feel more awareness of God at work in his creation than almost any other children of the church. This is one of the greatest blessings any Christian could ask for his children.

Very Close Friends

Probably no other subject is as difficult for the pastor as that of his friendships. Should he and his wife have very close friends among the families of the church? Especially in a small church? There are two points of view:

1. The pastor and his wife are human beings. They will not be able to develop themselves or the graces given to them by God if they do not have at least some families with whom they can socialize with total freedom. Also, there are times when things that are down deep inside just must come out; therefore personal friends are needed or these things will come out anyway, but to the wrong people.
2. Anytime the pastor and his wife make very close friends of one or two families in the church, the rest of the church

67

often worries that confidences may be broken (overtly or unsuspectingly) or that the pastor may be seeking advice and counsel (again, overtly or unsuspectingly) from these same few families about many aspects of his ministry. Thus these families become somewhat suspect by the rest of the congregation and the authority of the pastor may become tarnished or even undermined. Since most of the time people make the closest friends with others of approximately the same age, these dangers become magnified to those in the church who are much older or much younger than the pastor.

There is no simple answer. Experience shows that meaningful (but not necessarily limitless) friendships can be developed among the families of the congregation without fostering difficulty of any kind. One way to achieve this is for the pastor and his wife to seek several such relationships, not only the one or two that naturally "just happen" when Christian families get together. Furthermore, they should seek to develop the same kind of friendships everywhere possible, even beyond the immediate church. Also, they must carefully and graciously help their church friends understand the limitations they have chosen to put on the development of these relationships and seek to have mutual cooperation in this respect.

Finally, the fact that very close friendships are a problem for the minister and his wife makes it necessary for them to develop a constantly deepening personal walk with the Lord. The only ultimate solution to this problem is that, on a day-by-day basis, the minister and his wife find the burden of the Lord light and his yoke easy. This testimony will also be the best possible answer to any criticism that the "wagging tongue" might become unloosed.

Personal Appearance

The subject of the minister's personal appearance, the care of his body, and the care of his home merits attention. On this point two facts must be accepted by pastor and congregation from the outset: personal tastes differ and financial earnings differ. There is no such thing as a norm for style or taste, unless, of course, in the case of clothes the minister wears clerical garb. In any case, the minister never should permit himself or his home to look "grubby," rundown, unclean. There is no excuse for sloppiness or filth! Every pastor needs to take the time necessary to groom himself and care for his home (regardless of who owns it). The excuse that there is too much to do just will not wash; time must be taken for it.

The amount of money the minister spends on clothes and the home is important. Again and again he must seek a budget that shows careful planning, expresses his own personality, and fits naturally into his immediate situation. This budget will permit him to wear good clothes, have the freedom or the restraint of the custom of that area (cf. the casual dress of the Southwest to the more traditional dress of the Northeast), and permit his family new clothes without fear or guilt and without forcing them into any preset mold. The key is planning.

The same logic holds true for the house and its furnishings. However, if he must purchase his own house, his ability to obligate himself may be more or less than some in the church might expect. Whatever the circumstances, he should seek lodgings in harmony with those of the kind of people he anticipates reaching, even though his location may be different from theirs.

This subject also includes the need to keep one's own body in trim. Flabby or obese ministers and minister's wives do not speak well of the self-control that comes as a fruit of the Holy Spirit, whose work should be exemplified in every facet of the minister's life.

Bills, Credit, and Business and Management Matters

The minister must be able to hold up his head with confidence among the businessmen of the community. If he cannot, he may destroy his ministry. Consequently, it may be wise to seek professional counseling as to the use of money, especially at the outset of his ministry.

Occasionally the minister must ask for a loan. To do so he must establish good credit in his community so that he can borrow money when it is the wise thing to do. Two warnings are very much in order at this point. In the first place many ministers are not sufficiently aware that every time they use a credit card they are, in effect, taking on another loan, usually at about 18 percent interest per year. Overuse or foolish use of credit cards may well tarnish or even destroy a minister's credit rating. And such a bad rating usually will follow him for a good many years. In the second place the minister must pay his obligations on time. If he puts them off because he doesn't have enough money to go around, he is living at the expense of the merchants. If he doesn't have the money, he must curtail additional buying, cut down on other expenses (even if it really hurts), candidly ask the merchant for additional time, and pay additional interest.

Two simple rules will help in financial matters: never borrow unless it is an absolute necessity, and always know what the cumulative debts amount to before adding on more. A helpful practice to establish is to take time to understand all the mail about obligations when it arrives, and to file bills and related correspondence so that they are not forgotten or misplaced.

Several other areas of business and management must be mentioned.

1. Tax information. The rule is to avoid paying unnecessary taxes but never to evade paying proper taxes. The government makes certain tax benefits available just to ministers; in addition, because the minister is a self-employed person he must file income taxes and F.I.C.A. taxes; and tax shelter plans for retirement are very attractive to him. But the average seminary student and minister not only fails to appreciate these points but often seems almost unable to comprehend them on his own. Several specialized financial guidance companies dealing only with the minister's special tax problems are available to assist him. Needless to say, he should avail himself of them.

2. Correspondence. One of the greatest ministerial weaknesses is a failure to write letters. Frankly, many ministers are simply rude—they don't even have the courtesy to answer correspondence. Everyone who takes the time to write deserves the courtesy of a reply. And a prompt one.

But sometimes there is another problem concerning correspondence. It occurs when the minister appoints himself the church's official censor of appeals for help. There are two basic reasons why ministers do this. In the first place, many churches are flooded with such appeals. If the minister knows that the church has had no interest in the project in the past, usually he himself has no interest in it either; so he saves the officers or congregation the trouble of discussing it and deciding to throw it away by making the decision himself. The officers or congregation may never know that the appeals have been received. But even though he is right 95 percent of the time, the minister who takes this decision out of the hands of the officers or congregation sets himself up as the mind and conscience of his people. It will usually cause him great difficulty at some point.

The other reason for this censoring is much more serious. Ministers tend to protect themselves. In the first place, they protect themselves from the threat of the church overspending (so that they cannot pay the pastor). Secondly, they protect themselves from the threat of a new thrust of ministry which they don't personally like or which they feel they could not accomplish with their own gifts and graces. This attitude of being threatened will eat like a cancer at that minister's personal confidence and at his pastoral relationship with his people.

Whatever the cause for censoring appeals and the like, no minister is justified in taking unto himself this responsibility. The officers or congregation must set up the mechanics of acting on each appeal received, either directly or by delegation.

How to Live with Congregational Responsibilities

Prethink Options and Consequences

Among verses often taken out of context is Luke 12:11-12: "When you are brought before synagogues, rulers and authorities, do not worry about how you will defend yourselves or what you will say, for the Holy Spirit will teach you at that time what you should say." This verse does not give the minister the right to act as if he has no responsibility to be prepared before pastoral calls, before proposing ideas to his elders, etc. To act so changes the miraculous work of God into the magic of illusion. It always leads to confusion, often worse. Rather, the minister must think of each circumstance from every possible point of view, weigh the consequences, and be prepared for those consequences.

An example is in order. After leading a young woman to the Lord, a pastor tried but was unable to reach her husband with the Gospel. Several weeks later, the husband threatened his wife with grave physical violence and she called the pastor as well as the police. Before going, the pastor had to think through the situation from every conceivable point of view, such as legal, moral, family, and his own witness and testimony. As a result, he arranged for women of the church to stay with her at the home at least through the night so that he could spend time with the husband, first at the police station and afterwards at a motel. The option of spending all that time with the wife to comfort her (chaperoned by several women, of course) was thought through and discarded in order to demonstrate to the husband that he was indeed important in and of himself.

The practice of prethinking the possible events that might occur in any given circumstance is extremely important in preparing for congregational meetings and church officer meetings. Any such meeting carries with it the possibility of an unexpected comment triggering a chain reaction of comments that, in only a few minutes, can change the entire direction of the work or even destroy it. Many times the thrust of these unexpected comments would have been considered in a thorough prethinking session. Then the chairman of the meeting would not be caught with his guard down; he would already have thought at least of rudimentary answers and would thus have kept the control of the meeting in his own hands.

One way to use this concept when conducting meetings is to review beforehand the entire system of parliamentary procedure and review the constitutions and bylaws, the chain of command existing in the particular situation, and the mechanics necessary to use the bylaws properly when percentage votes must be determined. Another valuable practice is to rehearse all this data with the officers of the church before the congregational meeting so that they, too, have the details and mechanics fresh in their memory.

As a corollary, care should be taken that no major "block-buster" plans or ideas are developed by the pastor or one or two others ahead of time and then brought before the congregation or officers for the first time during a public meeting. Normally, one of two consequences will follow, both of which are devastating. In most cases, at least one or two of those present will have negative emotional reactions to first hearing the "block buster" in a public meeting. On the other hand, it is not unusual for congregations to respond by apparently "falling in line" with no reaction at all, only to demonstrate later that they really had not been moved to the degree of commitment needed to make the idea work once it was put into action. It is usually wise to present the idea or program informally ahead of time to several people in order to get opinions before it is publicly presented. Also, it is often very worthwhile to present the refined idea or program to the officers or congregation at one or two preliminary meetings where no formal action is possible, before presenting it at a meeting at which a vote is called for.

A second corollary is that one should so prepare for each meeting that the "blank-paper" approach never happens. Always come to a meeting with a docket, no matter how simple. In addition, always come to a meeting with your ideas thought out enough to have at least the outline on paper. The proposal can then be reworked, disposed of, replaced, or whatever. But, if there is nothing before the group, there is usually such frustration in getting started that nothing is ever accomplished.

Work in Concert with Officers and Congregation

The pastor is not one who strikes out on his own. In his labor of overseeing the flock he is a co-ruler with the other elders, not a unilateral ruler. He therefore needs the advice of his elders, particularly when *beginning* to deal with problems that later may need the participation of the elders or even the substitution of the elders for himself. But by that time he will have made it almost impossible for the elders to serve in any effective capacity, if he did not consult with them throughout.

It is of paramount importance that the pastor not proceed with his ministry without the prayer support of his officers and people. Granted, the prayer support may be weak and tenuous to start with, but it must be tangibly evident. He must recognize that the church is the people themselves, and that their support is essential to the success of his ministry.

Parallel to this is the need to develop new ideas and programs but not to go ahead unilaterally with programs just because they are needed. It is as necessary to use every opportunity to teach the people their biblical responsibility of submission to the Holy Spirit and consequent sense of commitment as it is to develop new programs.

Maintain a Liaison with All Age Groups of the Congregation

Each pastor more easily relates to certain age groups of the congregation (usually his own) than to other age groups. Still, he must maintain a concentrated and continuous ministry to everyone in the congregation. Through him, if in no other way, the valuable input of the various ages can be directed to the others of the church.

In this respect the pastor must make some effort to minister to the children of the church. From their earliest days they should be aware of his calling and ministry. One way to do this is by giving occasional object lessons to them in Sunday School. Many ministers have tried this, but felt they could not afford the time to assemble all the items needed for object lessons found in textbooks. A simple answer is not to approach the task by trying to get things together to demonstrate a given subject but rather to look for some subjective use of whatever happens to be handy—a hammer, fountain pen, needle and thread, etc.

Another way to develop this ministry is to review one's records about the children before visiting the home, directing some of the conversation during the visit to them in order to learn more about them, and praying specifically *with* them as well as for them.

The pastor must also maintain direct contact with the teenagers of his church no matter how many or few of them there are, and no matter whether it is an easy ministry for him or not. During these formative years of their lives they must learn confidence in and respect for the pastor. It might be wise to set up personal counseling times with them just to keep involved in their growth. Once in a while he ought to take them on a spiritual retreat, mingling with them in the many circumstances this affords.

Another facet of his ministry with teenagers is knowing them well enough to be aware of those who seem to have the gifts necessary to be ministers of the Gospel. When he does find young people who are thus blessed he should challenge them to seek the leading of the Lord in their lives about it. Of course, the pastor must be very careful to make judgments on mature assessment, not just emotional or circumstantial evidence. He should include his elders in the efforts to locate and encourage these young people. He must also realize that the Lord may take a long time to make his way clear to these young people—they cannot be rushed!

He must also find some means of ministering to the family units of his congregation. Some ideas often used are:

- couples' groups dealing with contemporaneous, probably controversial, subjects.
- routine visiting
- men's breakfasts
- women's activities

Finally, he must minister to the older people of his congregation. The pastor is probably more necessary to them individually than to any other age group in the church because of their special needs; therefore, he should have regular personal contact with them. He must also make a special effort to delegate this ministry to others in the church whenever he himself does not have time to devote to it, and not allow the elderly to be bypassed by default. This minimum expression by the church of its need for the senior citizen will help the elderly enjoy the dignity of their humanity and appreciate the beauty of their organic relationship to the corporate body of Christ.

A good rule of thumb to guide the pastor in the kind and quantity of relationships he must maintain with each age group, as the bare minimum of his responsibility, is this: At all times there must be sufficient pastoral relationship existing with each age group of the church so that any member of the church will always feel free to call on him if he feels he needs his help.

Special Church Activities

The pastor must develop a realistic sense of priorities between his work and the many opportunities that come his way for specialized, additional ministries. Almost every community will have some need for the minister's specialized service. Occasionally the requests amount to little more than a front to put respectability on a public event. Some occasions, on the other hand, offer the opportunity to bear a meaningful witness. He ought to be able to bear a greater witness by serving on a school board for two or three years than by bringing an occasional prayer at a service club meeting. He must not allow any of these opportunities, however, to overload him so that he is not able to fulfill his basic calling to his congregation. Decisions in this area require the advice, wisdom, and often consent, of his elders. The elders must always be aware of these decisions, whether or not they help make them. Very seldom, and only after much prayer and deliberation, will such service be in activities which, although acceptable in and of themselves, might prove to be an embarrassment to the local church.

One kind of specialized activity that may take a great deal of the minister's time is a committee assignment for his church's denomination or association. Ministers of churches with such relationships, of course, must devote a proper amount of time and energy to their denomination or association in order to maintain their responsibility. Experience shows that such service often becomes an obsession to some ministers, and an escape from local problems for others. Care must be taken for honest appraisal of the amount of time and energy necessary to this involvement.

75

Related to this subject is the need for the minister to distinguish between civil and ecclesiastical activities. Many times he should stand shoulder to shoulder with other citizens of his community for civil causes when he could not share equally with these same people in ecclesiastical matters. This distinction is not always easy to make, but must be thought through for the sake of the glory of God.

Conclusion

This chapter offers personal experience and advice. Some readers may not agree with all of it. Certainly many more subjects could be dealt with. I earnestly hope that the material presented will excite some serious thought about the responsibility of being a pastor of a flock of Jesus Christ's.

Part 3
THE CHURCH OFFICERS

6

The Making
of the Church Officer

The subject of church officers and their responsibility for over-seeing the congregation has been presumed thus far. It is now necessary to develop more fully the concept of the church officer.

In the first place, the Bible makes it abundantly clear that the church is a kingdom. Thus it has a king, King Jesus. He is also called the Head of the Body. He gives commands to the body—the church, the kingdom—that are to be obeyed (i.e., the Great Commission).

The church, under her King, is given the responsibility to govern herself. She does this by adopting norms from the Bible for church government and by depending on the guidance and assistance of the Holy Spirit. The Holy Spirit uses particular members of the church who demonstrate qualification for office and have been set aside by ordination (see Acts 13:3; 1 Timothy 4:14; 2 Timothy 1:6). This is an organizational procedure necessary for the church to be a functioning organism. It is impossible to have an organism without an intrinsic element of delegated responsibility.

Every church has one of three possible forms of government:

(a) hierarchical—i.e., the bishop controls ordination and there-fore the ultimate life of the church;

(b) democratic—i.e., the majority vote of the congregation de-termines the membership policy of the congregation, and occasionally the pulpit is counterbalanced by the diaconate in recommending direction to the congregation;

(c) republic—i.e., specific duties are designated to qualified members, with the congregation bearing ultimate control by determining who will be elected to office and how long they will be permitted to serve in office.

The following discussion will primarily benefit those churches of democratic or republic form of government; yet the matter of qualifications and responsibilities are applicable to every situation.

Definitions: Elder, Deacon, Trustee

Before defining church offices, it is important to note that the Bible, directly and by illustration, describes the work of the elders and deacons. Therefore, to the extent that elders and deacons do the work the Bible calls them to do, these officers have their authority directly from the Bible. Consequently, this authority is intrinsic to their office. That is, to ordain and install a person as an elder or deacon is also to invest him with the authority to do the job the Bible describes. However, there is nothing in the Bible about a trustee. Therefore, the office of trustee carries no intrinsic authority. Any initiating action a trustee takes ultimately must root itself in the designated authority specifically given by the corporation.

The elder: overseer of the church's spiritual pilgrimage. "They must be men of wisdom and discretion, sound in the faith, diligent students of the Bible, able to teach others, and committed to guarding the purity of the church. They should be an example to the flock in personal Christian living. It is their duty in conjunction with the ministers to exercise government and discipline and to take the spiritual oversight of the particular congregation. . . ."[1] This statement fits together the various Scripture texts concerning the qualifications and responsibilities of the elder. Since these texts have already been discussed at some length relative to the pastor as a ruling-teaching elder, they will simply be listed here. The major biblical sections are: 1 Timothy 3; Titus 1; 1 Timothy 5:17; 1 Peter 5; Acts 20:28; and Hebrews 13:17.

The deacon: a minister to the church's poverty needs. The deacons must also be men of wisdom and discretion, sound in the faith, and diligent students of the Bible. Again, they should be examples to the flock in personal Christian living. It is their duty to determine financial needs in the congregation and the community, to collect offerings to help alleviate these conditions, to distribute the funds (or goods), to use the occasion to teach biblical principles, to comfort and to encourage, and to act to prevent poverty wherever possible. Occasionally churches assign other administrative and charitable duties to them. The Scripture passages that deal with the deacons' qualifications and responsibilities are: 1 Timothy 3; Titus 1; and Acts 6.

The trustee: an agent delegated to do the church's bidding in its financial and real property needs. The trustees are often the elders

1. Standards of the Reformed Presbyterian Church, Evangelical Synod.

or the deacons or both together. On occasion the office of trustee is separate from any such overlapping. In any case, the trustee should have the same spiritual qualifications as the elder and deacon since he will be called on to be the representative of the church to the business community. As such, by the way, he may actually be the most visible representative besides the pastor himself. This in itself demands a high degree of spiritual maturity as qualification for the responsibilities of the trustee.

The Call, Training, and Election of Church Officers

In 1 Timothy 3:1, Paul indicates that the elder "sets his heart on being an overseer." The elder, and by implication the deacon, must therefore be someone who has given much prayer, thought, and time to considering this office and feels compelled of the Holy Spirit to serve in it if called on by the church to do so. Certainly he is not one who is given a job just to "keep him involved"! This text clearly implies that he is already involved even without the job. Also, to aspire to the office must mean he is already a living demonstration to the church that he is ready and qualified to serve. It must be remembered that the authority base for the eldership is the responsibility to rule so as to give a good account to God of the well-being of each member of the church. This takes grace. It takes a special work of the Holy Spirit. Therefore, true "desire" for this job must indeed be a gift of God in and of itself. Any other reading of this phrase implies that the candidate immodestly declares his aspiration, as if it were his ambition to be given a place of authority and honor. Yet such could not be the case, because it would clearly contradict Peter's list of qualifications, specifically that he has no right to "[lord] it over those entrusted to [him]" (1 Peter 5:3). There indeed is a call of the Holy Spirit to be an elder or a deacon, and the Holy Spirit's *modus operandi* is to motivate the potential candidate out of love and concern for the spiritual needs of the people.

The trustee has no reason to be "called" to his office, since there is no intrinsic biblical place for his task. He simply is serving the church so that it will be able to meet the laws of the state.

Nomination and Training

The training of the elders and deacons is a major task. It is most important that the training period be in the proper sequence of

81

events. It must be before the candidate's election, ordination, and installation into office. There are dangers if this sequence is not followed.

Many churches do not have any training period for their officers at all. Their assumption must be that "on the job" training is sufficient. This may work in some churches. But it fails to enable the church to review the qualifications of the candidate in the context of in-depth study; and it fails to enable the candidate to be so trained in the doctrinal position of the church before he takes office that his affirmation to the questions of ordination is really an intellectual and moral commitment. Still other churches put the training between the candidate's election to office and his ordination and installation into office. This embarrasses both the candidate and the minister if the candidate is found to be unqualified or is not able both intellectually and morally to give his affirmation to the questions of ordination.

The weakness apparent in these practices provides Satan a tool to drag evangelical churches into discord and even occasionally into heresy and apostasy. Too often these practices have led to the installation of officers whose basic qualification was nothing more than sincerity or whose oath of ordination was nothing more than perfunctory. When the elders and deacons do not have the qualifications and the intellectual and moral commitment to the doctrine of the church, anything that sounds more or less biblical and "tickles the ears" can usually be preached from the pulpit with the consequent destruction of precious souls.

The schematic diagram below illustrates the proper sequence of becoming an officer:

FIGURE 5

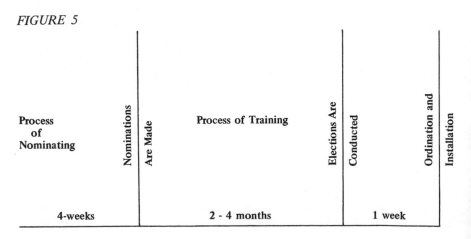

82

The first step is *nomination.* Before a nomination is made some study must be given to the general character of the potential officer's life, his fitness in the light of the biblical qualifications for office, and his willingness to devote the necessary time and effort to the office if he is elected. The second of these three facets of study must be done by the elders, often in lengthy personal conversations. A note of warning is in order at this point. In this prenomination assessment, the elders must distinguish between general knowledge of and agreement to the doctrinal position of the church, and the comprehensive knowledge of and agreement to that position that will result from the in-depth training program. The prenomination assessment is to be limited to determining that there is at least some knowledge of and agreement to the doctrinal position of the church, and to assess that the other qualifications for office are apparently present in each candidate's life. Since all of this will take time, the process of nomination should start at least four weeks before the training program. It is my opinion that the congregation should have a means to propose nominees, but the elders must have the ultimate authority to present the nominees or at least the list of candidates from among whom the nominees will be selected. It is also my opinion that the elders are obligated to present every name duly proposed for nomination unless the potential nominee clearly fails to meet one of the three standards indicated above.

This process of nomination has four implications:

(a) nominations will not be received "from the floor";
(b) nominations will be separated from elections by a training period;
(c) elections will not be possible at the time nominations are made;
(d) nominations will not be possible at the time elections are conducted.

The next step is the *training program.* There are several goals to be accomplished by this program:

(a) the nominee should be taught the material necessary for him to have a comprehensive academic awareness of the doctrinal and governmental position of his church;
(b) the nominee should be challenged in these areas both to a moral acceptance of them and the defense of them as commitments of his own;
(c) the nominee should be taught the duties of the office for which he is a nominee;

(d) the nominee should be taught the history of his local church (and denomination) with special emphasis on the specific distinctives of the church, so that he will be academically aware of and morally committed to them;

(e) the nominee should be helped to appreciate the strengths and weaknesses of the church (and denomination).

Each nominee certainly must read the entire text of the church's standards, both doctrinal and governmental, including the constitution and the bylaws of his particular congregation. The class training must be based on the assumption that all of this reading has recently been accomplished.

The training program curriculum for elders and deacons ought to begin by studying in depth the biblical qualifications for the office. Each nominee should be personally challenged to assess his own qualifications to serve if elected.

Next, the doctrine of the church must be thoroughly taught. This training must be complete enough to assure that the nominee has been challenged by the implications both of a broad view of the doctrinal position and of important individual points within it.

The same knowledge and challenge is necessary in the areas of government, history, and the condition of the particular contemporary church.

Finally, the details of the "job description" must be explained so that the nominee will be prepared to accept them as a moral obligation.

Following the training period the elders should satisfy themselves that the nominees are prepared intellectually and morally to submit to the ordination vows if elected. The nominees are then presented to the congregation for election.

As for trustees, in those churches where that office is not served by elders or deacons, it would do the trustees no harm to take the training course. At the least they ought to read all the standards of the church and to take the section of the training material covering the biblical qualifications for the elders and deacons. Finally, the elders should satisfy themselves as to the general character of life of each candidate for nomination and his willingness to serve if elected.

A workable formula for the training program is a two- to three-hour session, every other week, for approximately four months. Any block of four months will be interrupted by a special occasion (e.g., Christmas or Easter) so that the number of classes would probably work out to six sessions of two and one-half hours each.

If a nominee has taken the training within the past two years (for instance, if a nominee has been a deacon for a year and is nominated to become an elder) he need not retake the training course, but the elders should meet with him as to his attitude, among other things, before the election. All other nominees should take the course. The experience of incumbent officers will add a meaningful dimension to the class work, and the retraining will offer them a valuable opportunity to refresh themselves on the material, often sharpening their comprehension of it.

Next, of course, is the *election* by the congregation of elders and deacons and the election, by the corporation, of trustees in those churches which have a separate body of trustees. The rules governing the election must be incorporated in the bylaws of the church. The election most often occurs during the annual congregational or corporation meetings.

The Ordination, Installation, and
Term of Service of Church Officers

The ordination of an elder or deacon is a most solemn experience, both for him and the congregation. Examples of good questions of ordination are the following:[2]

1. Do you believe the Scriptures of the Old and New Testaments to be the Word of God, inerrant in the original writings, the only infallible rule of faith and practice?
2. Do you sincerely receive and adopt the doctrinal standards of this church, the Westminster Confession of Faith, and Catechisms, Larger and Shorter, as embodying the system of doctrine taught in the Holy Scriptures, to the maintenance of which this church is bound before God by solemn obligation?
3. Do you acknowledge the Lord Jesus Christ as the only Redeemer and Head of his church, and do you accept the Presbyterian form of church government as derived from the Holy Scriptures?
4. Do you promise such subjection to your brethren as is taught in the Word of God?
5. Have you been induced, as far as you know your own heart,

---

2. Ibid.

to seek the office of an elder (or deacon) from love to God, and a sincere desire to promote his glory in the Gospel of his Son?

6. Do you promise to be zealous and faithful in maintaining the truths of the Gospel and the purity and peace of the church, whatever persecution or opposition may arise unto you on that account?

7. Do you promise to be faithful and diligent in your personal and family life, as well as in the public duties of your office, endeavoring to adorn the profession of the Gospel by your life, and walking with exemplary piety before the flock over which God shall make you overseer?

8. Are you now willing to undertake the work of an elder (or a deacon) and do you promise to discharge the duties which may be incumbent upon you in this character as God may give you strength?

The ordination should follow election as soon as possible. It should be part of the worship of the church, probably at the next Sunday service. In many churches it is accomplished by the elders present coming forward and placing their hands on the head of the kneeling elder- or deacon-elect during the prayer of ordination. In some churches, however, only the prayer is used.

The installation is a declaration of induction into office by the pastor. The congregation is first challenged to pray for the elder- or deacon-elect, to encourage him in his duty, and, in the case of the elder, to express their agreement to be in subjection under him in his responsibility to rule over them or serve them so that he can give a glorious account to the living God. Then the pastor declares the elder- or deacon-elect to be installed into his office, and prayer is offered in his behalf.

Conclusion

All that follows about the work of the church officer is meaningless if the wrong person is in the office, or if a good person who doesn't understand, believe, and stand committed to his ordination vow is in the office. The opposite is not always just as true, however. The right man is still but a sinner saved by grace and he may make mistakes or even fail miserably under pressure. Nonetheless, the future strength of each church is directly proportionate to the caliber of those who, under Christ the Head—King Jesus—are the officers of the church.

7
The Elder: Overseer
of the Church's Spiritual Pilgrimage

Most ruling elders of evangelical churches take their calling seriously and do a commendable job of serving the Lord in their strategic post. The authority on which ruling elders base their ministry is, of course, identical to the authority upon which the teaching elder bases his ministry—responsibility to account to God for the sheep of the flock. In this regard the ruling elder is also an overseer of the church. This demanding responsibility, if taken seriously, either makes him an even more humble, praying man, or it may well break him. This chapter considers the application of this responsibility from all the aspects of a church's life, and assumes that the elder is indeed a humble, praying man of God.

Causes for Failure

Before proceeding into the discussion, it seems wise to point out some circumstances that cause elders to fail to be blessed and used by God. These causes of failure should be apparent to anyone, but all too often congregations choose someone not properly motivated to be an elder in the first place or not qualified[1] to be an elder, or do not permit the elder to exercise his responsibility after choosing him.

1. One kind of improperly motivated elder seeks the prestige that seems to be attached to the title. Needless to say, such motivation is not God-honoring. The properly motivated elder, rather than permitting any sense of prestige to attach itself to the office, will seek to let men see his "good deeds and praise [his] Father in heaven" (Matthew 5:16).

---

1. See Appendix E for table displaying the biblical qualifications in easily recognizable categories.

Another improperly motivated elder sees in the office a means to use the "know-how of success" from his personal vocation to make the church "get up and go." The properly motivated elder may well use all his "know-how"—and with real value—but he distinguishes between worldly definitions of activity and success and God's standards for blessing his Word and his people.

Ultimately such elders are doomed to fail unless their motivation changes.

2. Proper motivation, sincerity, and diligence are not enough to insure being blessed or used by God; in addition, an elder must be someone who can meet certain qualifications. A novice is one kind of person not qualified for eldership, and Paul deals with this specifically (1 Timothy 3:6). Yet time after time churches mistakenly place a man in the eldership on the premise that he should have a job in order to keep him involved. The Scripture declares if a person is qualified to be an elder he should be doing much of the kind of ministering work an elder does as a natural part of his life whether or not he ever becomes an ordained elder.

Furthermore, the novice is unqualified because he lacks the maturity necessary for gracious yet firm wisdom and leadership. The unseasoned elder, once given the power to vote, often becomes a dictator (see 1 Peter 5:3), which is far worse than having no elder at all for the church.

Another unqualified person is the one who does not exhibit some development in every category listed by Paul, even though he may be eminently qualified in most of the categories listed. For example, he may be very knowledgeable about the Bible or an excellent teacher yet not have his own children in subjection. Such a man will not be blessed in his ministry of eldership.

Still another is the one who seems to deserve the office because of his substantial contributions, his faithfulness to the church, or any of a dozen other worthy activities.

Finally, willingness to serve as elder simply because no one else wants the job is not adequate qualification. The willing person may be highly motivated, have high principles, sincerity, and deep dedication, but if he is not qualified he cannot be blessed or used by God in the eldership.

3. Elders who are not permitted to exercise the responsibilities of their office will not be blessed or used by God. One such elder is the "once-a-month executive." Elders called on to serve in this nonbiblical way usually are laboring to "direct" the church as if the board of elders was a board of directors of a corporation. As

such, they sit in a monthly meeting and evaluate reports on the church and set policies and plans for the church. They make decisions on the personnel to be hired or fired, assign jobs to church members, set goals for the pastor, and wrestle with financial needs. Occasionally they are called on to offer opinions or advice during the rigors of a disciplinary action. As "once-a-month executives" these elders are caught between their personal desires to be involved in experiences developing each Christian and merely conducting business decisions about Christians. Their reward is usually frustration.

Another elder of this type is the "rubber-stamp" elder. Whether he serves this way because he has no backbone or because he is dominated by the pastor or other elders or both, he demonstrates no meaningful influence on the church. *But* it must be pointed out that if the church begins to fail he carries the responsibility for failure before men and before God.

Before ending this discussion, it should be pointed out that although the logic of these conclusions is absolute, our gracious God has used some of these men in spite of their foolishness. Still, our biblical responsibility is to conduct the work of the church in obedience to his revelation, not to do his work in any way smacking of irresponsibility.

Relationships of Elders Within the Church

Two basic facets describe the relationship between pastor and elders. One is the historic Protestant premise of the parity of the clergy. The pastor is not several steps above the elders in authority or prestige; they are equal before God. For that matter, the pastor and the elders, though all are worthy of honor, are not the only first-class citizens in the congregation either. There just isn't any second-class citizen of the Kingdom of God!

This premise is important for several reasons. If there exists any sense of superiority of pastor over elder, the mutual love and confidence so needed to jointly shepherd and govern their flock is destroyed. A quasi-dictatorship probably will develop and ever-increasing tensions will take the place of love and confidence. Sad to say, this is true in many evangelical churches today, especially in independent churches. It must be corrected. The converse is true, of course, if the pastor is treated merely as an employee. The elders must appreciate the fact that the pastor is called by God and supported, not employed, by the congregation to be God's undershepherd in their midst. Else, when dissatisfaction arises about the pastor's ministry (as it probably will), the elders will be inclined to ignore the principles involved and solve the problem with their control of (or at least major influence on) the financial resources given to the pastor and his ministry.

The other facet of this problem is a misunderstanding of the so-called job description of the pastor. This problem was dealt with in chapters 1 and 2, so that simply mentioning it here is sufficient. Needless to say, if the elders expect the pastor to be doing one thing, while the pastor believes he should be doing something else, tension will soon develop.

On the other hand, when the relationships between pastor and elders are healthy, the relationships between the elders and the church itself normally are quite healthy and almost always very rewarding. That relationship of the elder to the congregation is unique. He must remember (see figure 1) that he is a part of the congregation, not a "director" over it, and he must exercise his office with regard to the everyday lives of the people of the church. He must be so involved, with gracious love, that he is accepted by virtue of his life rather than the prestige or influence of his office as an honored source of spiritual wisdom provided by God for the people of the church. With this relationship he will be able to serve. Without it, he will not.

The elders must be in constant rapport with the deacons, advising, encouraging, and, on occasion, even restraining them. This demands occasional joint meetings. It also demands respect and love that is easily discernible by deacon and church member alike.

Finally, the elders must also be in constant touch with the trustees, much the same way they are with the deacons (if, that is, the trustees are a separate group). Under the conditions defined in this book the trustee's reports to the elders will probably be minimal.

The Elder's Responsibility

The following description of eldership responsibilities is a discussion of principles, not a job description per se. The discussion is based on fundamental premises undergirding this book, namely:

- the church is "people," not an institution
- the church is both organism and organization simultaneously
- the service in office by elders and deacons is a function of the

MAJOR BIBLICAL TEXTS DESCRIBING
THE WORK OF THE ELDERS FOR THE CHURCH

CONCEPTS INVOLVED IN THE WORK	DESCRIPTION AND CONTENT OF THE WORK	SCRIPTURAL BASE FOR THE WORK
BASIC TASK	"Direct the affairs of the church"	1 Timothy 5:17
AUTHORITY BASE ON WHICH TO SERVE	"Men who must give an account [for you]"	Hebrews 13:17
OVERALL JOB DESCRIPTION (See Notes 1, 2, and 3)	Example to the Flock	1 Timothy 4:12 Titus 2:7 Hebrews 13:7
	Shepherd the Flock	Acts 20:28 1 Peter 5:1-4
	Oversee the Flock	Acts 20:28 1 Timothy 3:2 1 Timothy 5:17 Hebrews 13:17
	Guard the Flock (including rebuke, etc.)	Acts 20:28 2 Timothy 4:2 Titus 2:15 2 John 10-11

Note 1:
Note 2: Although these categories overlap each other, each has distinctive characteristics. These categories, despite their general description, provide the basis for directing the affairs of the contemporary church. For instance, administration of church programs would be an application of the overseeing of the flock; determining who can preach and teach would be an application of guarding the flock.

Note 3: This chart clearly demonstrates that the service of elders cannot be equated to a policy-making board of directors or an administrative executive committee, which meets once a month to do its business.

FIGURE 6

organism, even though the process of their selection was determined through organizational programming

A chart (figure 6, on the previous page) summarizing the major biblical texts that give instructions to the elders, introduces this study. The structure of the discussion will be to describe the responsibility of elders to care for each individual properly from the very beginning of his relationship to the church.

At the conclusion of this discussion a job description can be easily constructed by elders applying the delineated responsibilities to their specific church and its particular needs. However, this test will not provide the management the "know-how" needed to both administrate and shepherd without having too much for any one man to accomplish.

The elder's responsibility to candidates for church membership.

Two things should be said about candidates for church membership before considering the elder's responsibility to them. In the first place, joining a church ought never to be a requirement for enjoying its fellowship. Before any visitor becomes a candidate for membership, he should have attended long enough to appreciate and be enriched by the people and distinctives of the church. In fact, it may be wise for a prospective member to attend long enough to see ways in which he might be an enrichment to the church.

Secondly, the visitor to the church ought to indicate by his own volition that he believes he should be a member of the congregation. In other words, visitors seldom ought to be asked to join the church. The pastor, elders, members, and the written material provided by the church can make it clear without exerting any kind of pressure that the pastor or any elder would be happy to talk to anyone about membership.

Now, based on these prerequisites, the elders carry a particular responsibility to the candidate for church membership. They must enable him to assume his rightful identity and his responsibility as an integral part of the corporate body. This task of the elders begins with an orientation class. Many evangelical churches are content simply to rehearse several statements of doctrine and declare the training and orientation complete. Not so. The class should be geared to communicate to the candidate. This means it must be presented in just the right way for each person, not in a routine set of lectures as if church membership training were parallel to a "cooky-cutter" programming. The class should *introduce* the candidate to the following material:

- the doctrine of the church
- the government of the church
- the history of the church (local and denominational)
- the activities of the church
- the financial structure and needs of the church

Note the word "introduce." The purpose of the training program is to do just that, so the candidate has at least an intellectual knowledge of this material. He, like everyone else, will have to live with much of this material through various experiences of life before it becomes an integral part of his entire being.

Along with this introductory material must be an orientation to the specific personality (the "specific purpose") of the particular church. This will probably include arranging for the candidate to fellowship at least with key members of the congregation long enough to insure that the "heartbeat" of the church has been communicated to him.

It *must* be remembered that this training is a responsibility of all the elders, not just of the pastor. When this responsibility is shared the candidate will be aware of the concern of all the elders for him.

During the candidate's association with the church, and especially during the orientation period, the pastor must be making an evaluation of the credibility of the candidate's confession. There should be tangible evidence that the Holy Spirit has worked the work of regeneration in the candidate's heart—that he is indeed born again. Certainly the candidate must be able to articulate the conviction of his own salvation in his own words even if he does not use Bible quotations or standard clichés to do so. Also, the pastor must be satisfied that there are no evident transgressions that have not yet been dealt with before the Lord, and, if society is involved, before it. As an introduction to the elders' or congregation's consideration of a candidate for membership the pastor must express his conviction that the candidate's testimony is credible.

One way to involve both pastor and elders is to have the pastor teach the orientation class, but have the pastor and the elders (not necessarily simultaneously) develop the orientation work *in the home* of the candidate—preferably with the entire family present.

The candidate now should be ready to appear before the elders or, in the case of a democratic church government, before the congregation, to confess his faith and to show that he has a credible confession before men.

In addressing the elders, the candidate should be asked to testify to his salvation in his own words. During his orientation to the church, he should have been prepared for the fact that this would be expected of him. The elders must be aware of the tension the candidate might feel and be prepared to encourage him. On the other hand, the candidate should by this time have come to appreciate that his confession will build the internal unity of the congregation, and he should be willing to give this personal testimony both for the glory of God and to enhance his relationship with other members.

The candidate should also be willing to commit himself to be subject to the oversight and discipline of the elders. If he has not yet been baptized, he must be baptized in obedience to the command of the Lord.

Normally a church will enroll members by one of three methods:

(a) Confession of faith. This means that this is the first evangelical church he has joined since his conversion to Christ.

(b) Reaffirmation of faith. This means that he is, or at least has been, a member of an evangelical church but does not come into this church by letter.

(c) Transfer of letter. This means that he is a member of a sister-type evangelical church, and his membership is being transferred to the present church.

It should be apparent that the candidate will give his personal testimony in every case. In effect, then, the various methods of enrollment provide the data necessary for meaningful evaluation of the church. From this data a church can determine if there have been any confessions of faith or if all those joining have simply transferred from another evangelical church. The church that seldom, or never, is blessed with confessions of faith is a church that is probably seriously ill regardless of the number of people joining. A rule of thumb seems to be that at least 10 percent of the new members each year in a normally healthy church have joined by confession of faith.

In churches using the republic form of church government (for instance, Presbyterian and Reformed churches), the candidate is received into membership by the elders. This act is usually sealed before God in prayer. The new member is then presented to the congregation and given opportunity to testify to his faith (often by answering questions directed to him by the pastor). In churches using the democratic form of church government (for instance, Baptist churches and most Congregational and Independent churches), the candidate is received into membership by congregational vote. Again, this union is sealed by prayer.

Membership Governs Church Purity

This discussion has been developed rather carefully in order to emphasize the need for maintaining the purity of the local body of Christ. At first glance, it would appear that the evangelical church is a select group not open to everyone. In fact, that is exactly the case. Church membership is restricted to those the Lord has led to himself. This distinction is a reflection of Jesus' own statement: "I am the way—and the truth and the life. *No one* comes to the Father except through me" (John 14:6). All too often the line between accepting Christ as personal Savior and joining the church is blurred; after preaching the Gospel to the lost, many ministers issue an invitation to join the visible church as the response to the Gospel. But failure to follow up conversion experiences and to train potential members creates untold difficulties by giving the power of voting responsibility to babes (see 1 Corinthians 11 regarding serving communion).

Similarly, a threat to the purity of the local body of Christ is introduced by those churches who practice infant baptism but do not require the child, upon growing into maturity, to experience a credible confession on his own before giving him membership power to vote. Such a practice is not in accord with the covenant theology supporting infant baptism in the first place, and is a gross dereliction of responsibility on the part of the elders in the second place.

Finally, this discussion has been developed at this length to make it abundantly clear that a church that does not expect a credible witness by word and life from each candidate for membership is doing a dreadful disservice to that person. He may never again be at the point where the challenge to heart and life can be effective. After all, if an avowedly evangelical church already received him as a member, he has every right to consider himself to be evangelical and from that time on the issue is settled for him.

95

Responsibility to church members for their spiritual welfare.

(a) Responsibility for the church member to be growing in grace. One way to evaluate growth in anything is to measure the distance remaining to the goal toward which the growth is directed. The ultimate goal for growth in grace is, of course, to become like Jesus Christ himself; that is, to seek to be perfect. Jesus commanded us: "Be perfect, therefore, as your heavenly Father is perfect" (Matthew 5:48). However, if the Christian is not careful, he tends to visualize this experience as a life that is like a pyramid, so that he is actually getting to be more and more perfect. Actually, this is an incomplete concept based on an immature appreciation of the work of the Holy Spirit in the life of the believer. While it is true that sinful deeds condoned by the babe in Christ are more and more overcome, and while it is also true that spiritual concerns are more and more taking their place, yet to say that the Christian is therefore approaching the pinnacle of perfection is to be blind to the fact that his thinking must simultaneously include an upside-down pyramid! As he grows in grace, his understanding and comprehension of God, righteousness, holiness, sin, and temptation all will grow by leaps and bounds. Consequently, even while the Christian may be praising God for sins conquered, his very growth in grace simultaneously makes him ever more sensitive to his own standing before God and more aware of the love needed to save him in the first place and keep him thereafter. Therefore, to point to Jesus as the goal for the growth in grace for each church member is also to point the Christian simultaneously to a concern ever to purify his present life and a longing for the perfection of fellowship that eternity with Jesus will ultimately bring. It dare not be one without the other.

A second way to evaluate growth is to establish a starting point and at various intervals record changes, measuring the distance from the original point. To use this method, the elders need to know something about the growth of grace in a person's life at the point when he becomes a member. Granted, this is a subjective assessment; but it must be made. Actually, almost every mature Christian instinctively makes such an assessment about each new contact he makes anyway. Since the elders must have maturity of judgment in order to become ordained in the first place, they certainly should be able to exercise this judgment.

One of the first things to be evaluated, before a candidate becomes a church member, is his personal commitment to Christ. This is determined by assessing

- the degree to which his whole being is involved in personal fellowship with God
- the degree to which all the aspects of his life are based on his submission to the Lordship of Christ
- his knowledge of the Bible and of biblical doctrine
- his witness of love and graciousness, especially as evidenced by the relationships shown in his immediate family

The ultimate assessment of these facets of the candidate's life and faith is usually a composite opinion of the pastor and the elders. It will be a point of discussion between them in the formal meeting during which they will rule on his eligibility for membership. Since it should be part of every elder's nature to begin making such assessments the first time he meets anyone, this "formal meeting" is, in fact, a mature consideration based on in-depth associations, not just a mechanical listing of data. From this assessment the pastor and elders will at least recognize:

- major areas of disturbance or sin that will need much prayer and loving counsel
- personal problems that need comfort, encouragement, and sometimes financial help
- existing special programs in the church which would be a specific help at that time
- individual members in the congregation from whom the new member ought to benefit in special ways
- talents and gifts inherent in the new member that will be a blessing to the congregation

The ultimate use of this assessment should be a discussion with the new member to help him appreciate the love and concern of the church for him and the opportunity the church is challenging him to accept for his own life.

As the new members become older ones, the elders must make continuous evaluations of their growth in grace and counsel them accordingly. This demands some system of regular contact. Routine visiting is the usual and the best method. Individual elders may be assigned a certain proportion of the congregation on the basis of geography—those families living near an elder become his special responsibility.

Regardless of how this responsibility is carried out by the elders, the church member must be aware that the elder's concern is much more than an occasional social call to which is appended a Bible verse and prayer in the last sixty seconds of the visit. Historically, visits by the elders were occasions for the entire family to spend time together with the elder as he catechized the family. Such a practice still merits consideration under certain circumstances. Whatever *modus operandi* is used, at least the following matters ought to be discussed in an elder's routine visiting:

- the blessings church membership has brought
- any problems or disappointments church membership has brought
- the personal means the church member is using for his growth in grace
- the needs of the entire family, with special concern for possible decisions or problems that may be ahead for members of the family
- the needs of the congregation (spiritual, physical, financial) and what the church is doing about them

How, then, does the elder involve the pastor and the other elders in the consequences of such visiting? Obviously any emergency situation he providentially "stumbles upon" will demand immediate consultations. In the normal course of events, the elders should meet once a month and review for consideration and prayer one-tenth of the church roll at each meeting. (This leaves the two summer months free.) This practice may use a third to a half of an evening's meeting, but, ultimately, people is what a church is all about. Therefore, so be it!

The elder's second area of concern for spiritual welfare is:

(b) Responsibility to advise members during decision-making experiences. This is an area of ministry that all elders should be involved in but seldom are. All too often they are called upon to help rectify a situation rather than give advice during the process of decision-making that brought about the situation in the first place.

The entire concept of guidance (finding the will of God) is, of course, at the foundation of this ministry. Therefore, it is necessary to explain how guidance is given by God. Since guidance is the evidence necessary to decide upon one course of action as opposed to all others, and to have the confidence to believe that the chosen course is indeed God's leading, this discussion will be concerned with the way Christians (individually and as a corporate body of believers) decide what the will of God is.

Proverbs 4:23 is an excellent text upon which to develop this discussion. "Keep your heart with all vigilance; for from it flow the springs of life" (RSV—take time to study the context, Proverbs 4:20-27). Note that decisions flow from the heart, the seat of the emotions, the total person. This includes one's will, mind, conscience, emotions, and intrinsic knowledge of God, of beauty, and the like.[2] It is certainly not just from the intellect that one makes decisions.

The place to begin to find the concepts upon which to make specific decisions is the Bible. There are three fundamental points of reference for interpreting a Bible verse which will assist any Bible student properly to understand the Bible, regardless of the amount of education he has had. First, the basic teaching of the overall context must be understood. Among other things this demands a relationship of the context to the historical situation facing the writer. Then, the relationship of that particular verse to its context must be determined. Along with that goes the analysis of the grammar and words used, the style of writing being used, etc. Next, the verse, as thus understood, must be related to real and contemporary life situations to see what the consequences of the verse really are.

There are three kinds of contemporary situations to which the heart-searching of Proverbs 4:23 applies for testing one's motives and actions. The first occurs when one is faced with a moral decision. In this case, the heart has specific instructions in the Bible as to what decision to make. And there is no question but to obey the moral law of God. Deciding to obey God's law, regardless of the cost involved, gives the Christian the absolute assurance that "I am in the will of God." For instance, at one point in my life I worked in a large factory where most people took small tools and equipment home when they needed them. Even though I was laughed at and called "chicken," I knew that to take even a screwdriver or hammer was stealing, and I determined that I could not do so because the Ten Commandments make it completely clear not to steal.

The second situation involves the application of the major, fundamental doctrines of faith. Again, the heart has specific instructions in the Bible as to what decisions to make, and there is no question but to decide to stand committed to the fundamental doctrines of God's revelation. The end product of that decision is also the absolute assurance that "I am in the will of God." For instance, I was asked once to preach a funeral message and to

---

2. See A. A. Hodge, *Outline of Theology,* for discussion of the image of God from this point of view.

emphasize good works as the essence of Christianity. Since this concept had been the conviction of the deceased, it was thought that it should be the thrust of all remarks made. I offered not to deliver the message rather than betray what I clearly believed: "For it is by grace you have been saved, through faith—and this is not of yourselves, it is the gift of God—not by works so that no one can boast" (Ephesians 2:8-9).

The third situation causing the Christian to search his heart as he makes decisions is not so clear-cut as the first two. It is this third condition, which causes the most heart-searching, that Christians must deal with most often. It is also the category into which almost all church goal-setting experiences fall. It can be called "discernment-type decisions" and asks things like "Do I send my children to X Christian college or Y Christian college?" There is just no verse in the Bible to answer that kind of question. Obviously, whatever decision is made, the Christian will not be able to say, "I *know* I am in God's will," as he can in matters of morality and major doctrinal revelation. In the area of decisions based on discernment, a Christian must prepare carefully before taking one small step of faith, so that he can say, "I am *reasonably, by faith, within* God's will."

But how does one make this preparation? How does the heart determine these issues? First, the Christian studies the Scriptures that show the way God works in cases at least somewhat similar to his own and considers the advice of trusted ministers and elders of the church and other friends in the Lord based on their understanding of the Scripture and its specific bearing on his problem. Then, praying to be specifically guided by the Holy Spirit, he weighs the implications of the options that have become apparent through these two sets of stimuli. Finally, in a spirit of confidence in God, he must take a small step of faith based on the prognostication that seems most to glorify God while also answering his problem. The goal of such a decision in the area of "discernment" is to move from "dead center."

Special comment is needed to substantiate the idea of determining the likely outcome of each option. Christians often try to assess people, churches, institutions, and options the same way they assess the quality of a truckload of bricks. They look only at the condition of things directly before their eyes—always very carefully, of course!—and then decide they like this person and not that one, this option and not that one. When proceeding this way, Christians almost always find later that they didn't really have all the facts and are discouraged by the developments as they

GUIDANCE

"Keep your heart with all vigilance; for from it flow the springs of life" (Proverbs 4:23, KJV).

KIND OF DECISION TO BE MADE	INGREDIENTS NECESSARY FOR THE DECISION-MAKING PROCESS	DEGREE OF ABSOLUTENESS OF THE GUIDANCE PROVIDED
Decisions about moral matters	The heart, plus specific Bible verses	I can know: "I am in God's will."
Decisions about major doctrinal matters	The heart, plus specific Bible verses	I can know: "I am in God's will."
Decisions demanding discernment (All decisions not covered above)	The heart, plus Bible principles, plus advice from church elders,* plus saturation in prayer to be sensitive to the Holy Spirit's confirming that prognostication which seems most to glorify God, plus a single step of reasonable faith (* especially as to use of the Scriptures and to interpretation of the so-called open or closed doors)	I can at least know: "I am by faith within God's will." In some cases, especially very personal ones such as the choice of a marriage partner, the Holy Spirit's confirmation should be exceptionally clear. In all cases, the single step of faith is sufficient to bind each party to all moral commitments involved.

FIGURE 7

take shape. Actually, as soon as a Christian begins to assess options, institutions, or people, he must admit that he dare no longer make judgments from "static" data based on a quality-controlled "cross section of the whole." Rather, he must determine what general impression previously was made by this person or institution, what impression it seems to be making now, where it seems to be going, and what has motivated this progress. At this point he begins to develop a favorable or unfavorable prognostication.

By studying the direction of a person or institution and determining what motivates this direction, the Christian decides if he likes what the future apparently holds. A standard illustration is the reaction of stock owners when the bottom drops out of the market. Most stock owners see trouble for themselves and sell. But others, using the same data, must come up with a different prediction or there would be no buyers!

Let me point out that such goal-setting carries with it several additional but essential assurances: first, the assurances that presumption (having "faith in faith") has not been substituted for true faith; second, the confidence of being *reasonably,* by faith, *within* the will of God; and third, if things don't seem to work out perfectly, the assurance that this responsible dependence on our heart was the best reasonable step we could have taken with our finite and sin-cursed beings. God did not fail, nor was the Christian grossly out of God's will. Along with this last assurance, the Christian will consequently have the desire to learn from this experience so that under similar conditions in the future he will benefit by it.

Figure 7 (p. 101) summarizes this discussion by charting the kind of decisions to be made and the process of making them.

Having now discussed the basis of decision-making, let us note the responsibility of the elder in this regard.

- He must help the church members find the biblical passages that show God at work in similar circumstances
- he must offer mature advice based on his understanding of the Scriptures and suggest practical applications of them to the specific decision before the church member
- he must become an involved prayer supporter for the church member during this entire process

It is evident that such involvement soon makes the elders necessary in the personal lives of church members as well as in the corporate life of the congregation. Such involvement will develop an organism of love unsurpassed in human society—a living church!

(c) Responsibility to provide and to oversee the programs necessary for continuous growth in grace and for participation in the work of God. The elders have a responsibility for the corporate development of the body of believers. This does not mean that the elder must do everything himself. Indeed, if he does he is defeating his own purpose—he is depriving the church member of the blessing of serving God.

Further, a church's activities must fall within prescribed perimeters. The programs of the church are of two basic kinds: (1) those designed to present the Gospel to the lost (evangelism) and (2) those designed to enable the Christian to grow in knowledge and grace[3] and with the specific purpose of that church.[4] All the programs must have both individual and corporate worth, and each program must have a specific, tangible goal.

To carry out their responsibility, the elders must have a high degree of involvement in establishing, staffing, guiding, participating in, and refining the programs. They must seek out from among themselves, the pastor, and the people the creativity necessary to provide the constant growth and participation of the congregation.

In some cases they may find it necessary to do the actual work of initiating programs. This would be true, for instance, in recognizing the need for a church-wide Bible study conference. In other instances, the elders may merely need to guide the already motivated people in their planning. Coupled with the initial planning is the need to set a tangible goal for the program. It is in this regard that the elders must relate the program both to the universal purpose and specific purpose of the church and to the other programs of the church. It is true that sometimes the goal must be kept general until the program has had time to gel, but this ought to be the exception and not the rule. And even a general purpose must be in basic accord with the purpose of the church.

Any program needs personnel. It is a church axiom that someone must be willing to give himself wholeheartedly to a program to make it go. In all personnel decisions, whether for paid or

---

3. See *The Birth, Care, and Feeding of a Local Church,* chap. 2.
4. Ibid., chap. 3; see chapter 11 of this book also.

volunteer help, the elders must at least be prepared with suggestions and always have final approval.[5]

Any beginning program will almost always need guidance and occasional refining. Take a specific example in the experience of establishing a new church. At the outset a budget is provisionally adopted. For the first year it must be reviewed and revised every three to four months before it becomes meaningful. In fact, it then takes another two years of revision before it is usable in the formal sense of budgetary control. The elders, therefore, must anticipate close guidance of each new program during its early life.

At the same time, of course, the elder as a member of the congregation is actually participating in many of these programs himself and with his family. If a program has no value to him and his family, he should be alert to the possibility that it does not have much value to others either.

The elders must make regular evaluations of every program of the church. Such evaluations are made by comparing its present value to both the initial (or at least the most recent) evaluation and to its conformity to its stated goal. Many church programs monopolize a lot of time and energy without really accomplishing anything beyond the general goal of fellowship. They always existed in the past and no one wants to bear the onus of suggesting that the program be stopped. For instance, why does a church have a Sunday School? After all, it is not demanded (as are worship and the sacraments) by the Bible. There are, of course, excellent reasons to have a Sunday School. But if its value really boils down only to the fact that every evangelical church is supposed to have one, perhaps the elders should put a stop to that Sunday School, at least until a valid, tangible goal is adopted and the people are committed to achieving it.

A word of warning is in order about the gifts, talents, and skills of the church members, who, after all, will staff most of these programs. The elders must recognize that the Holy Spirit gives gifts to some people and special talents to others. These talents and gifts are for the edifying of the entire congregation, not for the edifying of the individual to whom they are given. They result in the ministry of the Spirit accomplishing salvation for the lost and growth in grace and knowledge and in vital organism among the saved. Therefore, the elders must use them.

---

5. There are many good texts dealing with the ways and means of choosing personnel. One is *Organization and Leadership in the Local Church,* by Jerry C. Wofford and Kenneth K. Kilinski (Zondervan, 1973).

But God has also enabled his people to develop certain mechanical skills, such as cooking and carpentering. Elders must be careful not to single out mechanical skills and urge them to be used as if they were spiritual gifts and graces. Mechanical skills may make possible a great blessing for the congregation—true. But if a good cook is always in the kitchen, or a good carpenter is always on the stepladder, they are not contributing much of themselves to the organism and hence are deprived of both giving and receiving grace through the body. As pointed out in chapter 1, the church is held together by the exchange of graces between its members (Ephesians 4:17), not by the exchange of mechanical skills.

(d) Responsibility for discipline. It is a sad commentary on evangelical churches that the practice of discipline is almost non-existent or (when man-made legalism becomes the norm) that discipline is practiced in a mechanical, rigid, even merciless way. Even in churches with a Reformed heritage, long a stronghold for biblical discipline, it is seldom practiced today.

One of the reasons is that the purpose of discipline is misunderstood. It is too often conceived of as the way a church decides whether or not a member is worthy to stay in the church. This concept is not only false but also in direct opposition to the Bible itself. Discipline is for the correction or prevention of evil within the church, and the restoration of the individual(s), not for putting people out of the church. True, the ultimate discipline is excommunication, but even that must result in the church looking upon the excommunicated person as someone to be won for the Lord by love and merciful compassion, especially by inducing him to a "godly jealousy" for what he should have but does not.

The meaning of the word *discipline* closely corresponds to the New Testament word *paideia*, and it is included in the broader concept of edification as expressed by such New Testament words as *paraklesis, nouthesia,* and *oikodome.*

When properly understood, then, discipline is for "the preservation of the purity and good order of the church (Acts 5:1-11; 15:1-13), for the spiritual welfare of its members (1 Corinthians 5:5), and for the effectiveness of its witness to the world (Romans 12:17; 1 Corinthians 14:23-25; John 13:35)."[6]

The use of discipline is so little understood that a New Testament example is very much in order. In the church at Thessalonica

---

6. The Book of Discipline of the Reformed Presbyterian Church, Evangelical Synod, chap. 1, para. 4.

some of the Christians had died. The church was keenly aware that the Lord could return at any time, and its members had apparently expected his return before anyone died. Therefore, there was the fear by those remaining that some of their loved ones had died too soon and would be left out of some of God's blessings for the Christian. Paul's priceless answer to that fear is found in 1 Thessalonians 4:13-18. However, a second problem flowed from this erroneous conviction. Some Christians decided not to work, but to "sponge off" the others for that short interval before Christ's return. Paul gave a gentle rebuke, which is "discipline," in 1 Thessalonians 4:11, when he admonished them to "mind [their] own business and to work with [their] hands." Apparently this gentle rebuke went unheeded, so Paul directed the church to apply disciplinary action in 2 Thessalonians 3:10-15. Note the impact—"Do not associate with him . . . that he may feel ashamed. Yet do not regard him as an enemy, but warn him as a brother."

If the apostolic church had to practice discipline, so do we!

In the New Testament, the primary sections that guide the church in its practice of discipline are: Matthew 5, 6, and 7 (the Sermon on the Mount); Matthew 18:15-17; and 1 Corinthians 5 and 6.

Almost every church will have some specific set of rules to follow in applying discipline. Some more general rules of thumb are:

- determine if the offense is such that it should be handled without any formal action (Luke 6:27-36; 1 Corinthians 6:7; Matthew 5:39)
- determine if the offense can be settled by private conferences and counseling (Matthew 18:15)
- advise anyone making formal charges that, if the charges made are proven unfounded, the person making the charge will be subject to the discipline that would have been meted out if the charge had been substantiated (Matthew 7:1-5)
- be sure, if a matter is to be tried by the elders, that anyone who is in any way connected with the problem disqualifies himself from serving
- when a formal charge has resulted in a formal discipline, that charge and discipline must be announced to the congregation in public

The value of discipline is that it tries to keep one out of jail in the first place, not just deal with the individual after he is in jail.

106

But true discipline, if it has been unsuccessful in keeping one out of jail, graciously and lovingly continues to work for restoration even during the incarceration.

Conclusion: A Church That Has the Right to Exist

This extended discussion leads to the conclusion that if God is blessing a church he will do so through biblical means, and the church and the world will see it, know it, and not be able to deny it. To put it another way, the elders must be prepared to stand before God and account for the existence of the church. No congregation dares assume that mere existence is sufficient cause for continued existence. Each congregation must have an awareness of its special mission and be able to see something of God's hand for good upon it. If it does not, the church is probably a comfortable source of personal blessing but not a challenge to personal growth. Such congregations are really only playing at church. This is the case with congregations that continue to drive into the midcity from miles and miles away to worship in the old building, in the old way, rather than move or serve the old neighborhood by doing whatever is necessary to reach the people. Or congregations become so devoted to gaining more and more detailed Bible knowledge that they become a clique of Bible students still calling themselves a church. The elders dare not permit these deviations.

Another facet of the church that must be alive and well, if it is to be worthy of continuing its existence, is its witness to the world around it, and, in particular, its application of the doctrine of the purity of the church to its witness. One-half of this doctrine has been carefully spelled out in this chapter, namely, the concern for the Christian to grow in grace and knowledge and to be used in Christ's Kingdom. The other half has to do with the corporate witness of the church, both as a specific congregation and, where denominational ties exist, as part of the overall denomination. When one or both cannot be a substantial witness to the glory of God, change is necessary. A church cannot give honor and glory to God if, de facto, the world looks at it and sees anything but a body of reconciled believers. In the case of denominational relationships, if the de facto witness of the association violates the Scripture, and if the attempts to cleanse and rebuild from within by discipline and program are consistently thwarted, there comes a breaking point, and the elders are responsible to recognize it. Second John describes the test of itinerant preachers in terms of commitment to Jesus Christ as God in the flesh. In fact, the church was not even to give them a greeting, "for the one who gives him a greeting participates in his evil deeds" (v. 11).

Elders, therefore, must supply leadership and oversight. They must conduct their ministry as though they might be called at any moment to appear before the living God to give account of the individual sheep of the flock and of the flock itself. They must be able to say to God, "By your grace our church is seeking to bring glory to your name."

8

The Deacon: Minister
for Remedying the Financial
Crises of Church Families
and for Acts of Mercy

The "diaconate" is a New Testament office. It is a specific office designed by God for the special needs of the church after Pentecost. Most deacons of evangelical churches take their calling very seriously. However, in spite of the high calling of this office deacons are often the most frustrated members of the church.

The deacon's qualifications are almost identical to those of the elder,[1] but most of the time he is relegated to four jobs—ushering, counting the offering, maintaining the building and grounds, and occasionally collecting food to give to the poor or to the Salvation Army to give to the poor. When a deacon has the maturity demanded by the scriptural qualifications but is never called on to put that maturity on the spot for the glory of God, he soon becomes disillusioned and frustrated.

It is true that each of the four jobs can, by stretching the imagination, be considered extensions of the concept of service to the people of the church. Disregarding for the time being the validity of such an extension, the fact remains that these jobs hardly ever utilize the maturity of spiritual life needed to be qualified for the office in the first place. Therefore, the very presence of such maturity brings the deacon to say, "What good is my serving this way—I'll carry out a more meaningful personal ministry without being a deacon rather than be a frustrated servant of God." This situation must be changed.

Some churches attempt to remedy the problem by normally electing elders from among those who have served first as deacons, thus making the diaconate a training ground for more responsible service later on. But this solution is totally inadequate. For one thing, deacons given limited responsibilities gain no experience

---

1. By comparing Scripture to Scripture, it appears that the qualifications are the same except that the elder must be "able to teach" and must be able to rule over the flock.

that would prepare them for the eldership. For another, many deacons never become elders, and are even passed over at times for a relatively new member who was an eminent elder elsewhere, factors that only add to, rather than mitigate, the frustration. Furthermore, all of the above make the office of deacon less than a high calling in and of itself.

Actually, the solution lies in developing diaconates that actively serve the Lord and his church in the special work of alleviating poverty and administering mercy, as the Bible defines their job actually to be.

The New Testament Office of Deacon

The deacon's job description comes from a composite of various Scripture passages. Acts 6:1-6 is presumed by most evangelicals to be the introduction of this special office in addition to the elders and apostles. Certainly the men in Acts 6 were set apart to relieve the tension existing in the apostolic church between the physical needs of the Greek-speaking Jewish widows and those of the Aramaic-speaking Jewish widows. These seven men are not called "deacons," but the related word *diakoneo* is used. Actually, they were "almoners,"[2] a term that describes a specific act of mercy by the church. Because of the existing tension, it took wisdom and spiritual insight properly to administer this food and also to bring glory to God from the church's new-found unanimity.

The New Testament does not have a great deal more to say about the specific office of the deacon. It is clearly implied in Paul's greeting to the church at Philippi (Philippians 1:1) that a formal diaconate existed by that time. Paul's list of qualifications for the office of deacon positively affirms the existence of and continued need for the office of minister to the needs of men ("deacon") for the New Testament church (1 Timothy 3:8 ff). Note that this list is couched in terms of wisdom and spiritual discernment, paralleling the context that demanded this of the seven deacons chosen and ordained in the apostolic church in Jerusalem (Acts 6).

A note is in order about 1 Timothy 3:11. I believe that this reference to women refers to the wives of the deacons. Regardless of the ultimate interpretation of this passage, however, logic and

---

2. See *The Book of Acts (The New International Commentary on the New Testament)*, by F. F. Bruce (Eerdmans, 1954), p. 130.

experience teach that, especially in the ministry of mercy to people well known in the church, the deacon's wives must often be the vehicles of administration because of the delicate nature of the problem producing the need. Therefore they must also have these qualifications of spiritual maturity.

One major truth about the service of the deacon comes through this entire study. The original seven were not simply delivery boys. These men were to use their office and the physical resources at their disposal to bring unity back to the local body of believers—to do a mighty and a spiritual service. But their ministry was limited to one area. Therefore, it is a logical conclusion that the diaconate, in the course of administering mercy, is expected to deal firmly with the causes and effects of financial crises existing in the lives of those they serve, not simply leave a basket of food for them. In fact, if all they do is leave some food, they demonstrate no regard for the problem of the people—they are treating the symptoms without also attempting to cure the cause of the trouble— therefore often producing an effect opposite the one desired in the first place!

To sum up, the work of the deacon is to alleviate physical needs (primarily of the people of the church) and simultaneously to minister to the causes generating the need and spiritual conse- quences resulting from the need.

Relationships Within the Church

Most of the time the pastor is an *ex officio* member of the diaconate. This seems to be the wisest arrangement (see figure 1, page 27, and figure 3, page 35). As such, the pastor is both a resource person and a safe guard person.

The pastor will occasionally have access to very delicate infor- mation about circumstances that will need both deacons' funds and, later, the spiritual ministry of the diaconate itself. In a bona fide emergency these funds must be made available to him upon request without waiting for formal approval. However, such occa- sions demand a previously agreed upon set of limitations and also a deep respect and rapport between pastor and deacons. It is nec- essary for both pastor and deacons to work constantly at strengthening these ties.

Furthermore, the deacons must be in constant touch with the congregation. Under the heading of "Responsibility," the me- chanical ways and means of accomplishing this communication will be described. For the deacons to be aware of needs that are either apparent or hidden from public view they must have a vital relationship with the people on a regular basis. Also, as representatives of the congregation, they must be cognizant of community or wider needs that demand Christian mercy, and seek to involve the church where possible.

Historically, one area of service by deacons beyond the local congregation has been the care, feeding, and immediate housing of Christians fleeing religious persecution and even assistance in finding employment for them.

The deacons are, of course, subject to the spiritual oversight of the elders of the church. The elders need to be fully aware of the extent of the ministry of the deacons in order to counsel and advise the deacons in carrying out their ministry, and to assure that the work of the two groups will be well coordinated. Ultimately, the deacons are part of the responsibility of the elders in their accountability to God, and the elders may occasionally have to prod the deacons on to a more active ministry or help them stay within the boundaries of their prescribed ministry, as well as counsel and advise them.

There really is no formal relationship between the trustees of the church and the deacons. In some churches the deacons may have to account for their funds to the trustees. This should not be. Where this arrangement does exist, efforts should be made to change it.

Responsibility for the Physical Needs of the Congregation

At this point it is necessary to relate the work of the deacon to counting the offerings and to maintenance of the building and grounds. Only by action of a congregation ought these tasks to be added to the work of the diaconate. If they are, it should be clearly stated that they are additional services accepted by the diaconate and that they will in no way replace the ministering acts of mercy or be allowed to become so burdensome that they infringe on that responsibility.

Actually, the church might well assign these tasks to others who are not ordained to the high office of deacon. They may function with full authority, within the limits of the budget adopted by the church corporation, and will be doing a necessary service for the church while enabling the deacons to be free for their own ministry.

112

The service of ushering has purposely been left out of the discussion thus far. Properly understood, this service could be considered a logical extension of the biblically defined responsibilities of the deacons, so that deacons would count it a privilege to provide this service as "coordinators of the worship service," however, not as ushers. Immediately it should become apparent that this task is not simply handing out the bulletin and bringing people to their seats. In includes:

(a) constant communication with the pastor to understand what he is seeking to accomplish through that particular worship service and what order of service he will follow;
(b) control of the flow of people into the sanctuary in such a way that the pastor's ministry will be most effective, especially as regards preservice quiet and meditation;
(c) control of the temperature and fresh air conditions;
(d) control of the needs of individuals who have special problems (hearing deficiencies, for example);
(e) control of the emergencies that occasionally arise, such as someone getting sick, a child or even an adult disturbing worship, calls for doctors worshiping in the congregation;
(f) provision for the pastor's wishes and needs to conclude the worship service in the way he feels led.

This ministry demands mature men, not novices. They *must* be granted time with the pastor before the worship begins and they may well pray with him before the service. These "coordinators of the worship service" are serving the Lord in very spiritual matters.

Responsibility—Deal with Financial Needs

Historically, this responsibility of the deacons has been considered under four interrelated topics:

(a) determining financial needs;
(b) receiving collections of money and real goods to distribute to those in need;
(c) counseling from the Scripture with comfort and advice and, when necessary, dealing with the basic causes of the financial needs;
(d) actively working to prevent poverty.

This discussion will develop these topics in the order presented above, but only, for now, as they occur in the local congregation. Community and worldwide needs will be considered later.

Determine Financial Needs. In "center-city" or ghetto churches, financial needs are painfully visible. In suburban churches they often appear not to exist. On the basis of appearance, many suburban churches have outreach programs along the lines of national welfare but nothing within their own church. Since there is no problem of identifying needs in the center-city or the ghetto church, this section of the discussion will deal with the suburban situation. But this is not to be construed as evidence of less concern for one kind of church than for another.

In the suburban church, the instances of financial needs are usually among certain groups within the church rather than "across the board." The most apparent places the deacon should check for signs of financial needs are the homes of one-parent families. If such a family is young and a large one, it will be difficult for it to live in small quarters and for the parent to leave the children in order to work. In due time, the family will almost have to move; yet the church often does nothing to help, often not even offering a simple "holding action" to give the parent time to get plans in shape. At the very least, church members could help with the actual move when it becomes necessary.

Another place to look is among the university and graduate students in the midst of the church yet away from home. When emergencies strike, their finely honed budget simply falls apart and very real need quickly takes over, especially if there is a child or two to care for. A special category of student is the foreign student who is preparing to go back to his own country well trained. Deacons should be aware of such students in the local church or sister churches and seek to help them on occasion.

Still another group who occasionally faces serious, often devastating, needs is that made up of young married couples who have never learned how to handle money and are literally on the brink of bankruptcy. The deacons must look for that need.

Every church sooner or later has a family (sometimes several) that has been permitted by God to go through sickness, sorrow, or natural disaster. Cooking, house and yard work, and "mothering" or "fathering"—as well as financial aid—may be needed for extended periods of time. In cases of natural disaster, homes may have to be opened for whole families to move in for extended blocks of time. The deacons certainly must be ready to cope with such needs when they occur.

Finally, and by far most often, there are the elderly, retired people who have to live on a fixed income, often little more than Social Security. They don't want to be a burden to anyone (after all, they were very self-sufficient all their lives!), and yet they just do not have what it takes to live in today's inflated economy. The deacons must look for that need.

There are almost always real financial needs right in the heart of even the most affluent church. The deacons must find them. To do so I would like to propose a rather novel suggestion for the work of the diaconate.

The elders must be so involved with the church people that they minister to them as true shepherds of the flock. However, the deacons must also be able to minister to the needs of God's people, or they are not qualified for office in the first place. Therefore, perhaps the deacons should also do regular, routine visiting to all the families of the church. This visiting would be to accomplish the following goals:

- find hidden cases of financial needs in order to respond to those problems
- find situations that could possibly lead to financial problems and assist those families
- sense the presence of spiritual problems and advise the pastor and elders
- minister something from the Word of God in each home

Such a program would demand close rapport with the pastor and elders, great spiritual sensitivity, and a commitment to the call of the high office of the deacon as a worthy service to God in and of itself. Such a program might even "turn on" the entire church for Christ. This kind of a visiting ministry seems entirely consistent with the high office of the deacon.

The need for such a high concept of service by the deacons was driven home to me many years ago in a harsh way. Plastic flowers had just become available. At a meeting of the diaconate, a discussion was conducted to determine if the deacons, serving as ushers, should wear a real flower or a plastic imitation flower to identify themselves. After an hour or more of discussion, one deacon left the meeting in disgust. He declared if that was all there was to being a deacon, he had better things to do. He left the church and almost turned against his faith. As a young pastor, I spent years anguishing before the Lord for this man and his family—especially since he was so right and the rest of us were so wrong about the incident that provoked his disgust.

Meet the Financial Needs. Sometimes money is needed. The deacons must have access to some funds with which to work in confidence. Often, especially in the suburban church, the need is of an emergency nature, and the only way to demonstrate fully the love of Christ and of the church is to be able to step into the situation with the means to help. Sometimes the need is for physical things, usually food. However, if a natural disaster strikes, or if sickness strikes a parent, the need sometimes is for total family care or for distribution of essential goods just to get started again.

Many of these needs can be met by regularly storing away money in the Deacons' Fund. Other needs can be prepared for by preenlisting families to respond to emergency appeals for food, housing, and the like. Occasionally the need may be far too much for such a standard kind of preprovision. Consequently, the deacons may have to make special appeals and collections. It is perfectly proper for them—under the oversight of the elders, of course—to do so in major emergency circumstances by house-to-house visiting of all the members and friends of the church.

After the collections are gathered they must be distributed. This is the specific responsibility of the deacons. It usually takes great tact and grace to do this in such a way that God alone is honored and that the recipient is blessed and not embarrassed or offended by being given the help. Often the deacons' wives must be the instrument of distribution because of the delicate nature of the circumstances.

Counsel, Comfort, and Advice from the Scriptures. The deacons are doing a spiritual work. Therefore, they must serve the needs of the people so that the physical gift itself is only a part of the spiritual truths taught through the occasion.

In doing this spiritual ministry, the deacons must be prepared to wrestle with the immediate problems to whatever extent is necessary in order to understand the underlying cause of the pressing circumstances. So long as that cause does not overlap the area of spiritual oversight (which must be cared for by the elders), the deacons must point out the real problem and the principles of Scripture pertinent to the situation.

In a great many cases, of course, the basic cause of the problem will be of such a nature (for example, insufficient income) that the biblical help to be offered is primarily comfort and exhortation. In addition, however, the deacons must demonstrate that the church does have a moral obligation to endeavor to give some physical help for the immediate circumstances and whatever help is needed to reach a long-range solution to the basic problem. In the case of insufficient income they must endeavor to find different or additional employment or some other means to increase the income, or education to use the available income to best advantage. It is at this point that the spiritual maturity required of the deacons, as well as their personal wisdom and influence in the business, commercial, and industrial world, will stand out for God's glory and for the help to God's people.

Work to Prevent Poverty. The two most obvious ways for the diaconate to work to prevent poverty are:

- teaching Christians responsibility in handling money, and
- actively expressing the concern the church may have about the development or decay of the community in which the church is located

In the first instance, little needs to be said other than to get to work and do it. Enough has already been said to show that every church—suburban, center-city, ghetto, or rural for that matter—has this need.

As to expressing the church's concern for its community, there are two areas to consider. In the first place, there are physical needs beyond the membership of the congregation that cannot be ignored. Most of them will be circumstances brought to the attention of the deacons by individuals in the church who have become aware of the specific need. In addition, there are projects within the community that are not related to the church but are worthy of support, such as a local Rescue Mission.

The other area of concern involves community trends and movements that will ultimately have a telling effect on the moral fiber of the entire community. In this respect, it should be noted that the incidence of poverty in a community is usually directly proportionate to the rate of increase in community decay of morality.

Further, it should be noted that this incidence really is directly proportionate to the inroads causing the community decay. A corollary to this is that the incidence of poverty is usually inversely proportionate to the development and the internal integrity of the community. This subject is a massive one and it has many implications beyond the purpose of this book. Therefore, several specific guidelines follow to start the diaconate thinking about the subject of community needs. (Guidelines are all that will be presented in this discussion, since each one of them is almost a major subject of research and study in itself.)

1. The evangelical church must relate at least to the sociological problems at its own doorstep if it is successfully to preach the Gospel to its own community.
2. The evangelical church must also be the major emphasis to declare that the chronological order for change given in the Bible is first to see men changed in their relationship to God and then to expect a change in man's relationship to those around him.
3. Community decisions must reflect respect for biblical standards of morality as opposed to pragmatic solutions that in reality are based on the heretical philosophy of "situational ethics."
4. The evangelical church must, at least occasionally and without feelings of guilt, spend individual and corporate time praying about community problems. Further, it must seek an internal unity of opinion about these community problems, even though these problems may be loaded with sociological and political overtones. Finally, it must be willing to take a public position on matters about which it has made conclusions.
5. The evangelical church must be prepared to acknowledge that it is proper occasionally to use some of its deacons' funds to assist in some community concerns which are programmed to prevent poverty.

Possible Additional Responsibilities: Comforting the Sick and Shut-Ins, Visiting the Member Families in Their Homes, Coordinating Worship Services, Devising and Operating the Missions Budget

Each of the items in this area of responsibility has often been considered a logical extension of the basic work of the diaconate. Great care should be taken about accepting this presumption as fact, as has been stressed earlier in this chapter. A few comments on these items, assuming the basic work of the diaconate is being carried forward, are in order.

Comforting the Sick and Shut-ins. When no financial needs are connected to the people of the church who are sick or shut-in, it is conceivable that this is not the deacons' work. However, it is so natural an extension of Christian grace that almost every diaconate practices this as part of their responsibility. I strongly concur with this practice.

118

General Visiting of the Families of the Congregation and *Coordinating Worship Services* were discussed earlier in this chapter.

Devising and Operating the Missions Budget. With the exceptions of building and grounds maintenance, this task seems the least likely extension of the biblical task normally assigned to the diaconate. Yet many churches choose to handle missions money this way. There are several dangers connected with this procedure, however, and they should be pointed out.

1. One danger is that giving to alleviate financial needs and giving to missions become almost synonymous, which, in turn, leads to the erroneous conclusion that missionary giving is really benevolence, not a direct outreach of the Gospel per se.
2. A greater danger is that the deacons so completely control the missionary funds of the church that the people of the congregation have almost no meaningful voice in directing the giving of the undesignated missionary funds of the church.
3. The greatest danger is that the missionary budget tends to occupy so much of the time of the deacons that they fail to administer their basic responsibilities to the full.

I feel that this is not a wise extension of the deacon's responsibility.

Conclusion

It must be apparent to the careful reader that the discussion did not cover the subject of participating in world-relief projects, etc. Certainly there is a need for the local church to respond to appeals of this nature. Such appeals, however, are almost always related to so many contingent circumstances that affect each church differently that it seems that the best advice is to consider each appeal separately and to test the proposed response against the church's standards of commitment.

Some of the material in this chapter may be a bit startling to most deacons. Few appreciate the high calling of their office. Therefore, much needs to be done to put the deacons back to work in the biblical use of their office.

9
The Trustee: The Legal Agent for and the Servant of the Corporation[1]

The office of church trustee is of major importance in the church and, consequently, of high honor. In all cases in which a nonprofit religious corporation is established, the office is authorized only by the civil government, thus distinguishing it from the offices of elders and deacons, which are authorized by the Bible. The office of trustee is the civil government's means of giving individuals responsibility over the real property circumstances of the church. They are responsible for the nonpersonal entity of the church.

If there were not agents authorized to represent the corporation, the only way a business could enter into a contract with the church corporation for goods or services (at least a contract of any size) would be to have every individual member sign the contract. Two corollaries of this are: (a) a business would not want to sue each individual if it felt the church had violated its contract; (b) each individual of a church would not want all of his personal estate open to such suit by virtue of his membership in the church. The trustees serve the needs of the civil government and of business in this regard and, consequently, they serve the needs of the corporation of people itself. The trustees themselves, however, are not personally responsible for the corporation's liabilities any more than any other individual member, except that they are indeed responsible for malfeasance or fraud.

The secular aspect of the trustee is even more apparent in a comparison of the ways by which church officers are authorized to act once they have been elected. The elders and deacons, whose

---

1. This discussion uses the term *corporation* throughout. The author is aware that different terms and slightly differing definitions are used by some states (for instance, in Virginia there are "trusteeships"; in Kentucky, trustees care for the financial needs of a church until it is incorporated, at which point the officers become the "directors" of the corporation). It is anticipated that the reader will make the necessary application of this data to his own particular circumstances.

authority base is the Bible, are empowered to act upon ordination and installation by the church. On the other hand, the first trustees elected by a newly incorporated church must have their names filed with and registered by the Secretary of State of the state in which the church is registered as a nonprofit religious corporation. And in many states subsequent trustees must have their names filed and registered before they can assume responsibility.

The Trustees' Basic Responsibility

Already the perimeters of the trustees' basic responsibility are defined. They are that the trustees of the church corporation stand as the legal agents for the corporation to the state and to business. Consequently, they stand as the responsible agents who assure the state and business, and the corporation itself, that the church's business is done decently and in order. As such, they have great force in the area of making recommendations and of restraining improper business transactions. As far as initiating major new financial commitments, however, their name speaks for itself—they only "hold in trust" for the corporation. They therefore use their authority for new commitments only when directed to by the corporation. As such, they are its servants.

Spiritual Testimony Connected with the Office

The work of the trustees often brings them into the most conspicuous, and possibly most influential, places of responsibility for the Kingdom of God in the secular world. Therefore, it is a fundamental premise that the trustees must be men of spiritual maturity and good repute. Consider the following arguments to substantiate the premise:

1. The Christian, and therefore the church, is wrong in presuming that the work of preaching, teaching, praying, witnessing, and the like is the sole essence of the true Kingdom of God and that material things, business contracts, and the like are somehow necessary burdens that the church must endure for the present. In the midst of a rebuke on arrogance, Paul makes a statement that puts everything in true perspective. He says: "And what do you have that you did not receive. . . ?" (1 Corinthians 4:7). If Paul saw physical

things and spiritual things as equally from God, then the church today cannot create a dichotomy that would separate material things from spiritual activities. And it follows that the officers (trustees) responsible for material things are more than necessary appendages that must be tolerated in order to accommodate civil codes.[2] The church, therefore, dare not look upon its material and physical circumstances as anything less than part of its total spiritual testimony. Nor can it consider those people who are set apart to carry the particular responsibility for this aspect of the church's life less than vitally involved in the total work of the church's ministry of being the visible evidence of the Kingdom of God.

2. To bring glory to God it is absolutely essential that the work of his Kingdom be carried on in ways that command the respect and praise of the church's community. The trustees carry the responsibility to see that this is indeed the testimony that the church bears.

3. The trustees are called on to make the business ties (except for very minor purchases with the community). These officers usually are the first and often the only flesh-and-blood church members that the business leaders of the community ever meet in more than a casual way. As such, the church trustees have unique opportunities to bear direct witness to the person and work of Jesus Christ.

The office of trustee does indeed have an integral involvement in the spiritual testimony of the church for God's glory. It cannot be considered lightly.

Relationships in the Church

The trustees of the church are usually in office by virtue of one of the following six governmental arrangements in a local church:

---

2. The positive thrust of this principle is illustrated by the individual Christian's tithes and offerings. When the Christian gives his tithe (10 percent) to the Lord for the church's ministry, his remaining estate (90 percent) is not *his,* per se. He is a steward for God over the remaining estate, since it is all from God, first to last. Even the 90 percent is part of the church's ministry of being the visible evidence of the Kingdom of God.

(a) the trustees are a group of officers separate from the elders and the deacons;
(b) the trustees are the elders and the deacons serving also as trustees;
(c) the trustees are the elders serving also as trustees;
(d) the trustees are the elders and others who are not deacons;
(e) the trustees are the elders and deacons plus others who are neither elders nor deacons.
(f) the trustees are the deacons also serving as trustees.

The relationship that the trustees should maintain with the pastor and the other officers depends, of course, upon the governmental arrangement of the local church. I am persuaded that the trustees ought to be the elders. In any case, the spiritual witness of the church must never be strangled by differences of opinion on financial resources for various programs. However, if the elders are to serve as trustees they must be efficient at delegating work and responsibility, or the mechanics of the trusteeship will absorb too much of their time and energy.

Whatever arrangement is adopted, it is necessary that the pastor be related to the work of the trustees as a consultant and safeguard person. It is also necessary that full communication on a regular basis exist between the trustees and the other church officers.

Job Description

The job of the trustees is to "hold in trust" for the corporation. This general phrase is normally understood to incorporate three areas of activity:

1. Inherent responsibility. Because of the responsibility the civil government places upon this office, the trustees must guarantee that the financial practices and obligations of the church are in decent and proper order. This includes:

   a. oversight of the bookkeeping and accounting practices of the church to see that they are being done properly and that reports are made to the corporation in a regular and meaningful way;
   b. oversight of designated giving so that the instructions of the donor are followed and that the gifts are not misdirected or "temporarily" misused even for virtuous reasons;

123

    c. oversight of gifts received for which donors expect to claim tax deductions so that all IRS requirements are met, even if meeting them means some gifts cannot be accepted by the church;

    d. oversight of all the obligations assumed by the church so that they are fully met, and on time, or that proper and satisfactory arrangements are made for alternate ways to meet the obligations.

2. Designated responsibility. There are two kinds of responsibility that may be designated to the trustees. In the first, the corporation may delegate to the trustees responsibilities of a routine nature,[3] for instance, the responsibility to maintain its buildings and grounds. The second is of a special nature, such as the authority to borrow funds in the name of the corporation, up to an agreed upon maximum, for purchase of land, for constructing a building, or for making major repairs, alterations, or additions to an existing plant.

3. Recommendation responsibility. The trustees may choose to make recommendations to the corporation about the annual budget, for example, or building plans or renovations. They must make recommendations about financial obligations, ways and means of making them and limitations on them, for all plans requiring large sums of money.

Dangers in the Misuse of the Office of Trustee

The greatest danger related to the office of trustee is that of assuming control of the church by determining the use of its finances and properties rather than merely holding them in trust for the corporation. The trustees must always be mindful that the corporation is "people," not just an institution or business, and that the will of the "people" must be determined and respected. Then, and only then, will they be "holding in trust." It is indeed a sad spectacle to find a church that has its entire ministry dominated by trustee control. Its spiritual life may be stifled and there

---

3. Each such decision in effect adds a new statement to the church's bylaws and must actually be an amendment to the bylaws, made in accordance with the provision for amendment. It is subject to revision or rescinding on the same basis.

may be a contest for authority between the "spiritual officers" and the "financial officers," which may end in an ugly division in the church.

The answer to this danger is for the church to seek before God constantly to appreciate the spiritual character of the physical aspects of the church and consequently of the office of trustee.

Part 4
THE CHURCH ITSELF

10
A Church with Vision

"Have you ever felt as if you were wearing yourself out on a treadmill? That's the way I'm beginning to feel about my church. We are always having one meeting or another. Sometimes five nights a week I'm driving some member of my family to a meeting at church! And that doesn't count Sundays! Yet I don't think the church is really getting anywhere. Maybe all the activity is really not all that worthwhile."

The man who said that is deeply committed to his church and much in prayer for God's blessing on it—a pillar of the church. Yet seeds of disappointment are evident in this comment. His church needs to set goals (in sequence of priority), put them into practice, and move off dead center before it wakes up and finds itself dead.

Goal Setting Is Necessary

Goals are ultimate objectives to be achieved. Each local body of believers calling itself a church certainly should have the ultimate objective of becoming what the Bible declares a local, viable church should be. Any group of believers meeting together for worship or Bible study without developing its entire ministry has not achieved the biblical goal of a visible church. Unless it sets that goal for itself and seeks to attain it, it may never be a church. Yet it is "the church," not simply a sincere group of believers meeting together for worship or Bible study, that will stand against the gates of hell. Therefore the ultimate objective of becoming a church in the biblical sense cannot be ignored.

The natural corollary to recognizing and admitting that every church should have this goal is that every church should have attainable subordinate goals as well. The church, therefore, may indeed accept as necessary the practice of setting goals, at least for the major areas of its ministry.

Yet, goal setting is occasionally questioned by the most sincere believers. It is questioned most often in the area of setting numerical goals of any kind—for instance, of proposing that the church set a goal of 10 percent net growth for the year ahead. The objection as usually stated is: "There is no mandate in the Bible that the church must grow. Therefore, to set such a goal is, to say the least, extra-biblical and certainly is a presumption on the work of the Holy Spirit!"

Therefore, it seems necessary to deal with this objection before going on.

When it comes to growth and setting goals, the Bible does clearly touch upon the subject even though it does not give examples of specific goals being set by one or another of the churches described in the New Testament.

The Lord sent his twelve disciples out (Matthew 10) to go to the lost sheep of Israel and to "... preach this message: The kingdom of heaven is near" (v. 7). He instructed them to seek success. If they were not welcomed, they were not to stay (v. 14). The same truth is taught even more emphatically by Jesus concerning his commission to the seventy-two he sent out (Luke 10:11-12). It is true that these verses also teach that the messenger would not always be successful. He nevertheless was to seek for success; he was *not* permitted to be neutral! Further, he not only had to seek success, he had to make an assessment of the results and he had to take action reflecting that assessment.

Again, there is the very command that Jesus himself gave: "You did not choose me, but I chose you, and appointed you, that you should go and bear fruit, and that your fruit should remain, that whatever you ask of the Father in my name, he may give to you" (John 15:16). It is not possible to conceive of Jesus commanding that we must go and bear fruit and insist that this can only mean the greater spiritual maturity of tangibly loving the brethren. Therefore, the Lord not only proposed that Christians approach the matter of witnessing to the lost by seeking to succeed, but also He ordains that they bear fruit. The parable of the sower of seed corroborates this conclusion. The important thing is not the "almost" fruit bearing of some seed, but of the numerically evident success of those seeds which fell unto good ground.

This is further corroborated by Luke 10:2: "And he was saying to them, The harvest is plentiful, but the laborers are few; therefore beseech the Lord of the harvest to send out laborers into his harvest" and John 4:35: "Do you not say, 'There are yet four months, and then comes the harvest"? Behold, I say to you, lift up your eyes, and look on the fields, that they are white for harvest."

The conclusions so far derived from these facts are that the church is to expect to grow, and that the growth will be in numbers as well as in spiritual maturity.

To carry the argument one step further, the words of Jesus during his prophetic discourse and his Great Commission combine to show that he has given at least one specific goal and it can indeed be numbered. In Matthew 24:14 he teaches: "And this gospel of the kingdom shall be preached in the whole world for a witness to all the nations, and then the end shall come." In Matthew 28:19a he teaches: "Go therefore and make disciples of all the nations. . . ." By comparing these verses, we see that every nation (which list can be numbered) on the face of the earth must be reached. Therefore, the nations never yet contacted (again, a number which can eventually be determined) must be a specific goal of the church.

Finally, the definition of a goal given above must be kept in focus: "goals are *ultimate* objectives to be achieved." Because of our human limitations, it is necessary to remember that the goal is ultimate and that it may be necessary to reframe our time reference or our specific number in the light of additional experience. When thus understood, the goals we set will continue to be incentives and "benchmarks"; they will not be a source of discouragement.

It is apparent that the Bible does at least clearly touch upon the matter of being goal oriented and upon setting goals, and the church has the right to set attainable subordinate goals for itself.

One church's goal might go something like this: "The goal of this local, visible church is to develop a visible branch of the body of Christ which is conformed as fully as possible to biblical revelation in doctrine, government, and life, and is capable of preserving its subordinate parts and the collective body itself during the church's development and thereafter." It is not the point here to discuss this particular statement of a goal but rather to use it as an example of a specific goal, the scope of which shows the necessity of having:

- vision—in order to reach the goal

- guidelines—to provide safeguards during the experience of reaching the goal

Vision Defined

The example statement has a key term in it: "to develop." For this development to become more than words, the church must have several things going for it. Mostly it needs vision to determine the subordinate goals and how to attain them. Vision is the ability, empowered with supernatural faith, to relate the present to the future by means of goals. Putting it more specifically, people with vision will:

1. initiate action by:

    (a) perceiving the future potential for the church;
    (b) expressing that potential in terms of goals;
    (c) spelling out those goals so that they will permit the church to be developed from its present stage of growth;
    (d) showing that these goals *are* necessary;

2. insist on combining commitment and responsibility with the supernatural grace of God to accomplish the goals;

3. inspire the rest of the members of the church to join them in stepping out by faith, primarily by showing their personal dependence on sovereign grace in fulfilling their own responsibilities.

Jeremiah was such a man of vision. He purchased land in Judah before the captivity because he intended to claim that inheritance afterwards, and he wanted the Israelites to be encouraged during their captivity by his conviction that he would indeed return and claim his property (Jeremiah 32).

A distinction must be made, however, between having vision and being a visionary. A visionary substitutes presumption for faith and expects magical achievement rather than the providential fulfillment of God's particular will through men of responsibility.

Goals—Their Criteria

There are three criteria to account for in setting each goal:

- *Goals must be biblical in context.* For instance, it is not biblical to demand a fixed number of conversions to Christ per year, nor is it biblical to consider conversions an impossibility and be content with none.
- *Goals must be measurable.* For instance, progress such as the

church's internal growth in Christ is measurable by personal testimony. On the other hand, a goal of seeing in one year at least one-half of the members become mature Christians is totally unmeasurable.

- *Goals must be reasonably attainable.* This prerequisite has two facets: size and time. For instance, it is reasonable to expect an infant church to start a meaningful missionary program of 3 to 5 percent of the undesignated giving of the church and to increase this by at least 1 percent per year for ten years. It is not reasonable to set a large fixed dollar amount to go to missions each year simply because that goal looks good on paper. A reasonably attainable goal, determined as "within God's will," will provide the measuring tools to assess growth. It will also provide the flexibility to redefine the goal without giving it up if the goal does not seem to be achieved.

Decision-Making Guidelines
in Goal Setting

The first guideline is to have the church admit that it needs specific goals. Sometimes there is a great difference of opinion about whether a goal is even needed, and if so, just what that goal is. If the church has voted to have a particular brand and model of church organ installed, there is no problem in setting the financial goal for gifts necessary to pay for it: determine the price and the goal is set. However, most situations require decisions that cannot be made in such a cut-and-dried manner—for instance, the decision whether or not to purchase the organ in the first place!

In circumstances calling for decisions based on mature discernment between various possibilities, goals are needed both to point out the direction in which the church should be moving and to provide a basis for evaluating whether or not it actually is moving. The mechanics of how to make such decisions were discussed at length in chapter 7.[1]

The next set of guidelines deals with setting priorities among the goals. As the pastor, elders, and congregation begin to set various goals, it will soon become evident that the subjects involved in them are so interwoven and so complex that the goals will vie with each other for the limited time and strength of the

---

1. A review of that chapter at this point is vital.

church. Therefore, they must be related to each other in a sequence of priority. This will efficiently use the resources of the church and, in some cases, avoid duplication or contradiction of goals. This concept is so important that no hesitancy should be permitted to deter recognizing the sequence of priority, adopting it, and then acting on it.

An easy way to do this is to establish three categories, one of which will fit any goal a church may set: (1) *highest and immediate priority;* (2) *necessary and eventual priority;* and (3) *unnecessary or future priority.* Any unreached goal in that first category should be troubling to conscientious church members. In order to avoid ungrounded guilt feelings, it is well to remember, especially in small churches, that no one can do everything—at least not at once!

The final guideline helps determine who is responsible *to make the goal decision in the first place.* It is paramount to remember that the church is the body of believers itself. Except and only in those areas of church decision delegated to the church officers by the Bible itself, or by the constitution of the church, all decisions should be generated from the people themselves, or at least must accurately reflect the mind of the people. For instance, in no way can it be construed that the Bible designates to either elders or deacons the responsibility of determining how much money should be spent on a church building program or what the church building should look like. Their advice is, of course, necessary. However, church after church has been split, with one splinter being "Deacon Jones's church," because one officer presumed so much privilege that he unduly influenced the church building program with his own ideas.

In summary, goal setting involves:

- admitting the need for the goals
- gathering the data necessary for deciding what the goals are to be
- actually setting the goals through the decision-making process previously described, using the prescribed guidelines

By now it should be very evident that goals *must* be set. Also, that they *must* be used. It is worse than an exercise in frustration to develop the habit of setting goals only to forfeit them by default or to forget them! To do that is tantamount to destroying the credibility of the pastor, the elders, and the church itself. Also, the church must be committed enough to evaluate regularly its progress toward the accomplishment of its goals. For example, one of the best ways to put life into the proverbially dead annual congregational meeting is to hand out the reports of the treasurer and the various society secretaries several weeks before the meeting and instruct the people to take them home and read them. Then, on the basis of the data already studied, spend the meeting time evaluating the progress of the church in reaching its goals, refining these goals, and setting new ones!

Finally, using goals demands a certain frame of mind. A goal-oriented person who sets goals, at least for his highest priorities, will seek the best way (always of a spiritual nature, of course!) to go around, over, under, or through apparent obstacles in order to attain the goal. On the other hand, a problem-oriented person will seldom approach goals with that zeal and drive. Rather, he will be tempted to say: "If we can overcome these problems, we will be happy to have achieved our goal," and may never get off dead center. Therefore, apply these ideas, set goals, use goals in the life of the church, evaluate progress, and give the glory to the Lord. It is reputed that Ben Franklin said: "Plan your work; then work your plan."[2]

---

2. See Appendix A for several actual goal-setting experiences described in detail.

11
A Church with a Specific Mission

The witness of Jesus Christ in the United States today is *not* dormant! Group after group of believers is testifying to the saving grace of Christ. The Gideons are spending millions of dollars putting the Bible into guest rooms and into the hands of servicemen; Campus Crusade is programming an evangelistic thrust to every American (Explo '72—100,000 people are into the program!); movie stars, such as, Pat Boone, are spending hundreds of hours "rapping" with teenagers and going on to baptize them by the scores in private swimming pools. And these are just a few of the examples.

Yet too few established churches are really involved either in a program of witness or in the development of newborn saints. A 1970 editorial in an underground paper among converted hippies on the West Coast summed up the need to overcome this laxity. The headline read: "Church—don't desert us! We have no other place to go! But—where are you?"

Discounting *all* the nonevangelical churches in the United States today, there are still plenty of local churches. What's wrong, then, that so many of them are not "with it"? Apparently there is a missing dimension in the evangelical churches of the seventies.

One frequent explanation of the missing dimension is that the church has not multiplied fast enough. "What we need are more churches!"

But this is not really the answer. Multiplication of something already failing only makes more failures, it does not change failure into success! The existing ills that keep contemporary churches from meeting today's needs are bad enough. But to multiply them usually just creates more frustration. On the one hand, the faithful Christian feels too guilty to admit failure and start over even though the new church does not develop as it is supposed to. And on the other hand, the new church becomes one more demonstration to those on the outside that the church has no answers for them anyway.

Another usual answer to the missing dimension is to develop programs for the church so that everyone is challenged to "get busy for God!" The concept is commendable, but experience shows that such programming usually succeeds only in leaving the already involved members totally exhausted, and the rest of the folks guilty, embarrassed, but still uninvolved.

Churches Project Differing Impressions

But not all evangelical churches lack that special element of success. Even among churches that have in common congregations made up of different kinds of people linked by their desire to be responsive to the Holy Spirit within the boundaries of biblical doctrine and government, some succeed in projecting an impression of vitality to outsiders, whereas others remain "just another church." What makes the difference between success and mediocrity, vitality and stagnation? Two things:

1. Whether spelled out or not, some kind of positive impression on the community is always made by the successful church, and this impression is made through combinations of five influential factors:

   • corporate worship
   • degree of concern for personal sanctification
   • programs
   • buildings and grounds
   • ultimate size

2. Whether or not the successful church describes its impression in these terms, it knows what kind of impression it wants to make on the community, and that, to make it, that basic impression (principle) is made evident in everything the church does.

It is my conviction that the only way a church will profit from this conclusion is actually to write out its own formal statement of such a principle and apply it to each of the five areas of influence listed above.

The missing dimension needed for the survival of the church, then, is this document, called the Specific Purpose of the Church.

The Missing Dimension: A Declaration of Specific Purpose

In one sense this declaration is a motivating principle. In another sense it is both a goal and a measuring stick. Primarily, though, it is a statement of the desires of a particular body of believers. It is the essence of what the entire church feels is necessary to be a viable, worthwhile local church, fulfilling the universal purpose[1] of any evangelical church. It is what the members believe must be their regular experience in order to:

- be fulfilled in their Christian worship and experience
- demonstrate that they indeed serve the living God
- successfully communicate the Gospel to their community

The declaration must be of such a fundamental nature that it has no smallness or meanness about it; it will not tolerate racial, financial, or academic barriers. It will give vital meaning to the entire life of the church.

The impetus for establishing new churches in the seventies illustrates the need for such a declaration. Most often, it seems God brings two apparently opposite kinds of people together. One of these is the formal, old-line traditionalist. He never wanted to leave his old church, but found that he could not go on being fed stones rather than bread and be, in effect, without a spiritual home for himself and his covenant children. The other is the progressive Christian; he was probably saved while a senior at a state university and may never even have gone to an established church. He may not own any clothes but blue jeans and pullover shirts. He probably knows a lot about the Book of Amos but almost nothing about the Gospel of John. He is spiritually stimulated by all-night bull sessions about the Lord and is active in witnessing to his peers. He has been used to lead people to Christ and suddenly finds that he needs a spiritual home for his convert children. And both have concluded they need corporate worship in order to be really fulfilled.

By providential circumstances these two apparent opposites are forced together in town after town. If they really mean business, it

---

1. In the beginning of every church a study of Ephesians is mandatory, especially the following verses, in the order given: 1:22-23; 3:10 (notice the present tense!); 2:10; 2:21-22. The universal purpose of the church—to reconcile man to God and to develop the consequences of that reconciliation in everyday life—is discussed in detail by the author in chapter 3 of *The Birth, Care, and Feeding of a Local Church.*

is not long before each of them makes a successive series of observations—sometimes admissions. They have both already admitted that salvation is a personal, individual matter, and that each individual's purpose is to glorify and enjoy God. Once thinking in terms of some kind of relationship, each ultimately discovers on his own that his personal need is *indivisibly* bound together by God with the existence and purpose of the church!

An additional conclusion (which they usually reach intuitively) is that the church of Jesus Christ is *indestructible!* The meaning of "until he comes" in 1 Corinthians 11:26, about the celebration of the Lord's Supper, now assumes new meaning. So does the meaning of Matthew 16:18: "And I tell you that you are Peter, and on this rock I will build my church, and the gates of Hades will not overcome it"; and of John 17:18, 21: "As you sent me into the world, I have sent them into the world . . . that all of them may be one, Father, just as you are in me and I am in you. May they also be in us that the world may believe that you have sent me." (Note the physical implications in all these verses; the church is not just an imaginary or invisible force.)

In the experience of learning to live together during the time these conclusions are mutually reached, the differences in these two types of people really begin to show up. The traditionalist begins to push for calling a pastor: "Let's get a pastor immediately. Let's get a topnotch preacher, with public relations experience, administrative experience, possibly some building experience, and he can get us *organized.*"

The progressive Christian takes a different point of view. He admits that they may need a preacher soon, but he declares: "We want a church where the members are not just bumps on a log; we want the people to be really concerned for one another, to be willing to take the time necessary to know and love one another so that they can admonish one another as part of Christian fellowship. We want a church where the people use their gifts, not just listen to the pastor. In other words, we first must become a living *organism,* then we can worry about being *organized!*"[2]

Now when these differences are considered on their merits and not just in an emotional context, each person begins to see that the church needs to be *both* organism *and* organization, not one or the other.

Ephesians 4:15-16 teaches this truth in a marvelous way: "Instead, speaking the truth in love, we will in all things grow up into

---

2. For definitions of these terms refer to chapter 1.

him who is the Head, that is, Christ. From him the whole body, joined and held together by every supporting ligament, grows and builds itself up in love, as each part does its work." The body has a head, but it is a growing organism, and it is held together in its growth in Christ by the supply of one part to another.

Peter deals with the same truth in 1 Peter 2:5: "You also, like living stones, are being built into a spiritual house to be a holy priesthood, offering spiritual sacrifices acceptable to God through Jesus Christ." As a stone house, the church is an organization; as a living house (consisting of living stones), it is an organism.

Now these two kinds of people begin to take a new look at some well-known Scripture. For instance, 1 Corinthians 12:13-27 comes to life as a biblical picture of the church as an organism. Acts 14:22-23 comes to life as describing a church being organized.

Having been brought this far in learning to love and appreciate one another, the traditionalist and the progressive Christian then must decide either to go it alone in spite of Scripture or to go it together because of Scripture. Those who decide to go it together next admit that each must contribute to the other and each must be ready to receive from the other. Through the experience of talking and listening to one another, a specific position emerges upon which they develop their church. This position is not necessarily "dead center" between them. It is the essence of what the entire body of believers feels is necessary to be a viable, worthwhile local church. It expresses what fulfills each one's need to be blessed as a part of a corporate whole; it shows that the church does indeed serve the living God and that it is successfully communicating the Gospel to their community.

In other words, these people have decided that they must have a declaration of specific purpose toward which to point their church.

Benefits of the Declaration of Specific Purpose

The drafting and the use of a declaration of specific purpose must affect the church both as organism and as organization. If only the organization is dealt with, the experience will prove to be devastating. However, if all the members actively participate in the entire process, their soul-searching experiences of supplying the data for the drafting of the declaration and then adjusting to the declaration that is drafted will effectively involve the organism as

140

well as the organization. Henceforth it will be assumed that both the organism and the organization have been involved in drafting the declaration and that the benefits described are affecting both the structure and the life of the church.

The most apparent result of drafting and using a declaration of particular purpose is to unify the church's activities around one central thrust. This is both good and necessary, and often this alone brings quick and impressive changes. But this is not enough. The declaration of specific purpose must provide a source of spiritual nourishment and challenge for the individual church.

Answer to Humanism

A less obvious benefit is to enable the local church to answer better the humanism that underlies almost every aspect of our culture. No matter how varied the trends and factions in our society may be outwardly, when examined closely they almost all reveal the basic assumption of humanism: man is an end to himself; the only meaning to life—or the absurdity of life—is to be found in man's own mind or body.

When Jesus Christ called himself the way, the truth, and the life, he left no room for humanism, no possibility for basing a way of life on man's desires or abilities. And every evangelical church knows this and probably stresses it to some degree. Yet few churches seem able to break through the expression of humanism they find at their own doorstep. Churches whose pastors regularly make a point of the supernatural character of the Gospel cannot fully overcome the unconscious acceptance of humanism by Christians, let alone stop (or at least restrain) the almost universal acceptance of humanism as the fundamental ingredient in the sociological, political, and academic work of the community and state. This is true because even the best sermon only illustrates, but cannot demonstrate, that faith in Jesus Christ is life itself—is at one and the same time the motivation for, the practice of, and the ultimate end of all life.

The solution, therefore, must involve more than sermons stressing the truth of the Gospel, although the solution is impossible without such preaching. The solution must encompass ways and means, in submission to the work of the Holy Spirit, for the entire church family to live this supernatural truth, both individually and corporately, in every facet of the church's life. Only when this happens will the church demonstrate its Christianity in a way that

141

will overcome the force of humanism. This means the church must orient its entire life to show Christ, not humanism, as life's answer, and to show this specifically to that particular expression of humanism at the church's own doorstep.

A church has thus faced its local situation, has sought an effective way to accomplish in its particular locality the universal purpose for which it exists—the work of reconciling God and man. Thus the development of a specific purpose has produced a meaningful benefit.

Enables Churches to Change As Communities Change

Another benefit provides the means by which the church can change as the community changes. Forty or more years ago city congregations almost universally responded to the challenge of changing communities by voting to move to the suburbs, and they did so without much of a twinge of conscience over the community that they left. In the last five to ten years congregations without a declaration of specific purpose have often splintered because of differences of conscience over this problem. The result of this splintering has usually been one of two sad experiences. In some cases, there has been a reluctant retrenching of a faithful few in the old building, attempting to do something in their changing neighborhood. The rest scattered. In other cases, the church moved, but was unable to take a full cross section of the congregation with it. Again, many scattered. Churches with a declaration of specific purpose will have faced the principles involved in such a situation before a specific circumstance demands some action. And when they act they will more likely make decisions based on principle rather than on emotion.

Enables the Church to Grow with the Community

Still another benefit of the declaration of specific purpose is to enable the church to relate properly to its growth and workloads. The experience of churches in the last ten years shows that congregations without a specific purpose tend either to be stagnant or to have a mercurial kind of up and down growth experience. If they have a particularly dynamic pastor, they usually respond by rapid growth. If they don't, especially for more than a three-year span and under less than dynamic leadership, a church's membership

142

often sinks to only those loyal to the church (in reality often loyal only to the church building!), or to those held by family ties, or to those who enjoy a high degree of close camaraderie and fellowship with others in the church.

The church that has a declaration of specific purpose will benefit because of the pastor's special talents, to be sure. However, Paul tells us: "He . . . gave some to be apostles, some to be prophets, some to be evangelists, some to be pastors and teachers, to prepare God's people for works of service, so that the body of Christ may be built up. . . . Instead, speaking the truth in love, we will in all things grow up into him who is the Head, that is, Christ. From him the whole body, joined and held together by every supporting ligament, grows and builds itself up in love, as each part does its work" (Ephesians 4:11-12, 15-16). The declaration of specific purpose will show how this relationship will involve pastor and people working together, regardless of special talents a pastor may or may not have.

Pursuing this thought further, Paul's words show that each individual whom God has provided for the church must be involved in contributing to the whole church, and that each one must anticipate being blessed by the contribution of the others. These contributions will be to the entire church life, not just to one or two aspects of it. When the pastor is able to minister in this atmosphere, the church will indeed be blessed and the growth will be of the Lord (see Acts 2:46-47).

Enables the Church to Make a Meaningful Impression
on the Community

A final obvious value of the declaration of specific purpose is that it will enable each church actually to project to its community that particular impression it feels called on by God to make. Since it is going to project an impression anyway, why not the particular impression it wants to project—that specific impression it believes most successfully demonstrates why it exists and how it intends to accomplish its purpose for existing?

Analyzing the Statement of Principle

The statement to be drafted will go to the heart of vital and often very personal concepts and standards. Consequently the members must be committed to a wholesome and Christlike attitude in relating to each other. This involves a basic disposition on the part of all to appreciate all members as necessary contributors to the work being done. Drafting a declaration is, in effect, coming to a consensus of opinion. Unlike decisions based on doctrinal or moral issues, or those based on a spontaneous reaction, this is to be a decision calling for discernment. As such, there *must* be the admission that the Holy Spirit enables each member, through his own personality, his individual background and training, and his present walk in life to see issues on an individual basis, and that the entire congregation needs the cross-fertilization of ideas that results from meaningful discussions.

The Congregation Must Know Itself Before Proceeding

The task of drafting the declaration demands self-assessment by the congregation. The members, of course, want the church to be a blessing to them, not only as individuals but also as a corporate whole, as the body of believers. This, in turn, demands that the body of believers assess itself in order to come to know what the corporate whole, the congregation, really needs.

The essence of what the members believe must be their regular experience in the church, in order to fulfill the universal purpose of any evangelical church, can be distilled into three statements mentioned above and worth repeating:

1. each member must be fulfilled in Christian worship and experience;
2. each member must be confident that the church is clearly demonstrating that it is serving the living God;
3. each member must be confident that the church is successfully communicating the Gospel to its community.

This self-assessment, this coming to know and understand itself as a corporate whole, may be started by using a questionnaire or by brainstorming the key concepts involved in the declaration.[3] Either experience could easily become a comedy or a tragedy if not handled correctly, and a stumbling block if not interpreted correctly. For these reasons it is wise to have a competent outsider

---

3. See Appendix B: "How to Brainstorm," and Appendix C: "A Sample Questionnaire and Schematic Survey of the Procedure of Drafting a Statement of Specific Purpose for a Church."

serve as a consultant. The pastor of the church, for instance, ought not be the consultant. If he were to assess the data in a way that did not happen to please some of the members, they would be tempted to think him unobjective. Therefore, outside, sympathetic but objective consultative help is almost mandatory.

Another precaution that cannot be taken for granted is the necessity to develop a strong content-oriented prayer base upon which to support the self-assessment. This prayer base *must* be continued throughout the entire program. Experience makes it painfully evident that the assessment can become an exercise in frustration (possibly even destruction) rather than edification when the prayer base is insufficient or when it is not fully maintained.

"Community" and Evangelism Related

Before giving an example of answers given by one church to questions about the three statements above, the word *community* must be understood in its fullest sense. And the relationship of this word to evangelism must also be understood.

The normal use of the word *community* by a church is the geographical or regional area in which the church is located and to which the church probably will direct its evangelical outreach. An additional meaning of the word must also be used by a church that is really concerned to be evangelical, and especially by a church developing and using a specific purpose. This definition is: people who have the same community of interests as the members of the church. To put it another way—those people with whom the members of the church most naturally and easily would make friends.

Now the entire concept of evangelism must be brought into focus, or else this second definition of community will lead to a church that in effect is a "closed circuit," the kind of structure that soon draws the comment: "Oh, *that* church! It's a clique if ever I saw one!"

Evangelism is a many-faceted ministry. It is effectively started, at least, by Christians worshiping and living in love one with another, so that the world is unable to escape the fact that all in the church are born again by the grace of God (John 13:35). This basic ingredient must be accompanied through lives of the church members (Matthew 5:16) by their evident encouraging one another to be "hungering and thirsting for righteousness" (Matthew 5:6). These facets of practical Christianity will permit even the

145

greatest novice or the most nervous, self-conscious person to communicate at least socially with his neighbor and, when possible, arrange for the pastor or an elder to visit the neighbor and explain "The Way" in specific terms.

This basic premise, therefore, leads to the conclusion that every Christian must in some way witness for Jesus Christ to his family, friends, and even his casual contacts.

Now as the Lord uses this personal ministry, some will be saved and eventually added to the initial core of believers. Their contribution will automatically enlarge the premise upon which the "community of interest" definition is originally based, thus keeping the declaration of purpose a dynamic force, not a sterile, static base leading only to a "closed circuit" congregation.

However, experience shows that new contacts from every member's circle of family and friends are limited after the congregation first commits itself actively to evangelize. True, each new member will have his own contacts, and he must be encouraged to attempt to reach them. But beyond this, who else should be reached? And how? This country is long past the day of exciting strangers to come into an evangelistic service simply by putting up a big sign saying: "Welcome to Evangelistic Services." The stranger normally never comes unless he is invited personally or, in some cases, if the topic or speaker appeal directly to a major thrust of his life. Here the concept of using the "community of interest" as the base for outreach is the breakthrough needed to reach beyond the church member's personal circle of family, friends, and contacts. *Community* can then be defined as a body of people, living where they have easy accessibility to the church's place of meeting, all of whom have some major aspect of their lives in common with each other.

For example, a church located in a university community brought in an evangelist who presented three messages on "Hell: A Real Place." No new people attended. Several months later, following my suggestion, the church brought in another evangelist. His theme was "The Meaning of the Mosaic Authorship of the Pentateuch." He stressed the impact of Christ's message to the rich man in Luke 16. The thrust of the messages was the same as that of the first evangelist. Each night new people attended. This church, primarily university oriented, had determined their own "community of interest" and evangelized on that premise.

As these new people were subject to the work of the Holy Spirit in their lives, several of them were born again and became part of the congregation. Their contributions to the church added still more to the premise upon which the "community of interest" was originally based. This, in turn, continued to keep the church a dynamic, not a sterile and static, body of believers.

An evangelistic program, if it is to be valid, must constantly use both of these outreaches simultaneously. And the new convert must be a contributing "joint" in the body (Ephesians 4:16) if the church is to be dynamic.

An Example of One Church's Answers
to the Questions Pinpointing the Three Key Truths

Now we can consider the way a local congregation expresses its own personality in their fulfillment, service, and communication. The congregation, or its elders, or a cross-section committee of the congregation, must express precisely its understanding of these truths. (For a church of more than a hundred people or a church with very apparent differences of opinion about these matters, the elders should always do this work.) In order to draft this expression, a questionnaire must be devised,[4] the answers to which will provide the necessary material. Below is my synthesis of one church's answer to an extensive questionnaire.

1. To be fulfilled:

    a. We must be constantly challenged: as to our daily practices, as to the wisdom needed in making decisions, as to the activities of our church.

    b. Coupled with that challenge, we must be aware of limitations and restraints, even chastening. Our public meetings must therefore show a sense of decorum. Our interpersonal relationships must therefore preserve a sense of decency in every respect, and concern for each other's personal sensitivities.

    c. The impact of these answers must be related especially to our regular worship services, our teenagers' needs, and our church's responsibility in the sociological struggles of our day.

2. To demonstrate service to the living God:
    We are not ashamed to declare that Christianity is a supernatural faith; our God is indeed at work in the world today.

---

4. See Appendix C for a sample questionnaire.

147

Therefore, we want to be very active in the experience of prayer coupled with a commitment to step out on faith wherever that is not confused with a step of presumption. In everything.

3. To successfully communicate the Gospel to the community: Our lives are primarily involved with our families and their needs. This concern includes the possibility of starting a Christian school. It looks for activities that include, not exclude, children. It also includes contemporary issues that will affect our families.

Drafting the Statement of Principle[5]

Now the statement itself must be drafted. This statement is an integration of all data plus a synthesis of the previous answers. Usually as many as three to five options will result, and the congregation must choose the one it really wants.

To draft this statement a special committee probably should be formed. This committee has four sets of data with which to work:

- all the data of the in-depth survey [6]
- all the results of the brainstorming session or the questionnaires
- the synthesized answers of the basic truths
- statements of preconceived goals prepared by members of the congregation

The following concerns should be reflected in the finished product:

1. Care must be taken that each major concept be expressed as a statement of principle; these statements must be practical and expressed in such a way that they are easily comprehended.
2. Care must be taken that sufficient data and illustrations be given to make these principles relevant for future study.
3. Care must be taken that the data and illustrations presented simply illuminate the principle and do not appear legalistic.

At a duly called meeting of the congregation, the various op-

---

5. See Appendix C for a sample questionnaire and schematic survey of this procedure.
6. See *The Birth, Care, and Feeding of a Local Church*, chapter 5.

tions for a principial statement are to be presented. (It might be wise to have copies distributed several days before the meeting.)

One option must be chosen. Refinements should be proposed and the amended draft be adopted as a provisional statement of principle. This provisional action will give some freedom for further refinement as the statement is applied, but it will not permit it to be principally changed without the consent of the entire church.

This provisional statement should probably be in force for two or three months after a statement relating the basic principle to church life has been provisionally adopted (see below). Then, at another duly called meeting, the statement of principle and the statement concerning church life should be formally adopted as the complete declaration of particular purpose.

The Previous Example Synthesized

Here is the finished statement of principle based on the above example of one church's answers to the three basic questions:

> This congregation shall constantly strive to saturate everything about itself in specific prayer, with a commitment to be seeking innovative and creative approaches to all aspects of its life, so long as they are biblical; and it shall consider the needs of the family as the basic unit of the church's life and development.

Preparing to Draft the Statements
Concerning the Factors of Influence

A small committee that is representative of the church should be established to draft a succinct statement concerning each of the areas of church life that contribute to the overall impression a church makes. These statements will be the application of the principial statement to the five influential factors mentioned at the beginning of the chapter. (The combination of the statement of principle and the application of it to the five factors is, of course, the complete declaration of specific purpose of the church.)

In this discussion of the statements, considerable effort has been made to analyze many aspects of the church. Through this extensive analysis, it is my intention to stimulate the committee to do something of an exhaustive study on each of the factors of influence. The result should be that the committee will produce such a wealth of material that it will serve the church many times over as a reference source.

Guidelines for the Committee

The following principles are guidelines for drafting each statement:

1. The principial statement should be interpreted, not expanded.
2. Each statement must not only be harmonious with all the other statements but must complement each as well.
3. The composite of the statements should be a practical guideline for all to use. This "all" includes:

   (a) all the various age groups of the church;
   (b) all those coming into the church later and thus not having the benefit of participating in the brainstorming, the drafting, and the adopting of the statements.

4. All the data already available must be used as direct resource material. The committee cannot content itself only with summaries or interpretation.
5. It may be helpful to compile illustrations of the statements. If so, it is suggested that they be added as an appendix.
6. The committee must study the sections of the doctrinal standards of its church pertinent to each topic as it is considered.
7. The concepts must be both idea oriented and reasonably attainable. This all-important guideline implies two dangers to be avoided:

   (a) the danger of being content merely with a synthesis of the best that each person remembers from past experience;
   (b) the danger of being so theoretical and idealistic that it is humanly impossible even to approach the goal in practice.

Experience has shown that it is often best to employ a consultant to assist the committee in its work.[7]

---

7. See Appendix D, "The Consultant."

Step-by-Step Analysis

Worship

The statement on worship will probably require more formal study than any of the other areas. First and foremost must come the definition of worship. My definition is: "In his worship, whether public or private, the Christian's total being seeks to adore God in response to his grace. While the worshiper is thus glorifying him, God in turn blesses the worshiper by fulfilling his spiritual being. This blessing carries with it the additional benefit of making it a joy for the Christian to live in obedience to God."

Along with agreeing on a definition of worship, the committee must study the doctrinal standards of its church and should take the time to study both Ezra and Nehemiah from the point of view of public worship. Finally, the committee ought to study several of the outstanding textbooks on the subject.

At least the following aspects of the worship service should be discussed by the committee before any statement is drafted:

- the purpose of worship
- the designation of the stated services of the church and the time each should begin
- the order of worship
- the place in the order of worship for the sermon and the purpose of the sermon
- the kinds of sermons to be delivered
- the kinds of music to be used (e.g., the variety, the quality and quantity of hymns, and special music)
- new methods in worship

The difficult part of the task is to take all the ideas thus far expressed, plus the data already compiled, and relate them to the principial statement.

The first result is usually a very awkward set of statements. They will, of course, have to be refined. It may be necessary to structure specific illustrations in an appendix so that the draft will adequately cover the subject and also be usable.

Degree of Concern for Sanctification

The statement on personal lives deals with the most subjective of all the five factors. The basic question is: What does the church expect eventually to see in the lives of its members as a demonstration of the work of the Holy Spirit in their midst? The answer is a study of the evidences of the doctrine of sanctification at work.

Two extremes must be avoided:

1. The subject must not be bypassed on the premise that, if God really is at work in the church, the evidence will automatically be demonstrated. A careful look at the Scriptures shows that the Lord told his own that they had responsibility for growth (see Colossians 3).

2. Sanctification must not be treated as if it were a list of "dos and don'ts"; such a list would have the effect of equating spiritual growth with legalistic achievement.

There are four basic areas involved in this subject:

1. Each member must more and more die unto sin and live unto righteousness. Each is "to say 'No' to ungodliness and worldly passions, and to live self-controlled, upright and godly lives in this present age" (Titus 2:12; cf. Romans 12:1-2; Matthew 5:16; Galatians 5:16-24). Note that this involves change.

2. Each member must become more and more aware of two needs:

   (a) the needs of others in the church—"If one part suffers, every part suffers with it; if one part is honored, every part rejoices with it" (1 Corinthians 12:26);

   (b) the need to witness to the lost all around him— "Therefore, since through God's mercy we have this ministry, we do not lose heart. Rather, we have renounced secret and shameful ways; we do not use deception, nor do we distort the word of God. On the contrary, by setting forth the truth plainly we commend ourselves to every man's conscience in the sight of God. And even if our gospel is veiled, it is veiled to those who are perishing. The god of this age has blinded the minds of unbelievers" (2 Corinthians 4:1-4a). Note that this too involves change.

3. Each member and the church corporately must grow to the place of steadfastness to the faith—"contend for the faith

that God has once for all entrusted to the saints" (Jude 3). Note that this also involves change.

4. The church must be corporately responding to the Word of God and the Holy Spirit so that it is indeed becoming (for even the world to see!) a dwelling place of God—"In him the whole building is joined together and rises to become a holy temple in the Lord. And in him you too are being built together to become a dwelling in which God lives by his Spirit" (Ephesians 2:21-22). Note that change occurs here too.

Obviously the essence of sanctification is change by growing into Christlikeness. The healthy church will have:

- the unsaved coming as onlookers, some of whom will be saved and become babes in Christ
- babes in Christ, who must be loved, protected, and fed, most of whom are growing into spiritually mature children of God, yet are developing at differing rates and hence are scattered over the whole spectrum of spiritual growth
- mature children of God who in turn assume more and more responsibility to proclaim the Word of God, so that
- still more unsaved are coming as onlookers

Thus no statement can be drafted that presumes all the people of the church will be more or less at the same level of spiritual growth at the same time. It should be pointed out, however, that this *is* the presumption of a great many evangelical churches. For instance, many such churches never hear a sermon on any other subject than salvation.

This discussion has related each point to the Bible. This was necessary for documentation, but it also shows the centrality that must be accorded the Word of God.

Again the committee will have to relate all of its available data to the material presented in this discussion on the concept of change. It may be necessary to differentiate between change in heart attitudes and cultural mannerisms. But very probably the core of this statement should be about change, based on knowledge and comprehension of the Bible; change for the individual and, to some degree, the corporate body, and change that epitomizes the thrust of the principial statement. Note, too, that this statement will bear directly on the statement on programs. In a sense, this statement is goal oriented; that statement is activity oriented.

Programs

The statement concerning programs could be one of the most controversial. The principial statement should demand that the church plan each of its activities thoughtfully and with a view toward fulfilling a definite purpose, rather than have a specific program (such as a women's circle) simply because "every church has one."

There are two basic kinds of programs:

1. Those for the growth of the Christian and his family. This includes, of course, the activity of every organization in the church (e.g., the Sunday School, young people's groups, and couple's clubs).
2. Those for reaching the lost (e.g., evangelistic campaigns, personal witnessing programs, and missionary involvement).

It is true that several standard church activities could be considered as belonging to both (e.g., the Sunday School, the women's missionary society, and the Summer Bible School). But I feel that many evangelical churches do not have any meaningful outreach to the lost. They think they have outreach as a part of the Sunday School and young people's groups. These programs often are successful in stimulating growth, but in reality they are not successfully reaching the lost. Note how few join the church by confession of faith compared to the numbers joining by reaffirmation of faith!

Certain circumstances must be considered by the committee before it can draft a statement about programs:

1. If the population is transient, certain programs will have to be repeated regularly in order to orient new people.
2. If the population is dependent on industry that uses shift labor, there must be constant adjustment of schedules.
3. If the church plans to use its facilities throughout the week (e.g., for a Christian day school), the scheduling must be manageable.

Before analyzing this material, specific thought must be given to the work the pastor is expected to do in the church, since his responsibilities relate him in some degree to every program of the church. The programs of far too many churches are no more successful than the pastor makes them. We dare not automatically accept this fact as biblical. The committee must give serious consideration to the concept of the pastor's office as described in chapter 2.

When the committee begins to draft its statement on programs, it will need to apply the principial statement to the data from this discussion. Often the easiest way to do this is to list the programs that are basic to the church and write a short description of each, enunciating the particular emphasis desired. (Later this material can be used as a detail in an appendix.) The final statement may then be synthesized from these short descriptions.

Building and Grounds

In dealing with the fourth factor, building and grounds, the committee must concern itself with goals, not details. It is not the purpose of the committee to consider construction details *at all* (as, for instance, proposed building costs or methods). The questions to ask if the church does not have a building should include:

1. Must the congregation have a church building in order to fulfill the principial statement?
2. If not, what are the viable options?[8]
3. If so, must it be of a certain architectural style?
4. Does the principial statement lead to multiple use of the building, especially during the week? If so, does that make the need for the building more urgent so that its construction becomes a priority item?

If a church building is indicated, its design is important. Too many evangelical churches tend toward one of two extremes as they consider the building and apparently cannot be made to accept any other position. One of these extremes makes the church as inexpensive as possible. Behind this thought is often the fear that it is unspiritual to spend money on anything other than the most functional, inexpensive, minimal design that would fit their needs. Consequently, the building is a cinderblock parallelogram, flat roof, with the walls of the church either left bare, white-

---

8. Some of the options already suggested or that I agreed to in special cases are:

    a. Rent college facilities for use on the Lord's Day.

    b. Buy a large house and remodel as the church building and pastor's residence.

    c. Rent joint space with a church of different practices.

washed, or stuccoed. From this viewpoint, an ornate building would appear almost blasphemous. However, this view fails to take into consideration the fact that the pile of cinderblocks says just as much to the passing public as does the ornate building. The unregenerate person seldom appreciates the frugality of the people; he simply is reminded of a commercial "chicken coop," not of a place of worship.

The other extreme position is that the church must be of colonial architecture, even if the best the members can afford is a very poor imitation. This view again fails to see the building as the unregenerate person would. He would probably see anything other than an architectural triumph of true colonial style as an unsuccessful attempt to "keep up with the Joneses," even though the church cannot afford the tastes of the Joneses!

The committee may want to wrestle with the building concept for their people in their location enough to be able to advise what general architectural style might best fit their needs and what the possible consequences of that decision might be both in the near future and for the long-range program of development.

The committee may want to develop its thinking about the matter of buildings and grounds simultaneously with its work on the last factor, the proposed ultimate size of the congregation. Needless to say, the projected growth pattern of the church seriously controls the size of the plant. This in turn seriously affects the architectural concepts that will be involved.

Again, it will be the task of the committee to bring together the principial statement and the data from its discussions. Often this statement will have generated extensive discussion, yet must be more general than the first three statements drafted.

Ultimate Size of the Congregation

The final subject, the ultimate size of the congregation, bears heavily on the structuring of everything about a church; yet it is usually not seriously discussed until the church is well established. Some commitment is needed from the very beginning so that programs, building developments, financial commitments, and the attitudes of the individual members about present and future responsibilities can all be productive.

The preceding discussion touched on the relationship of size to the building program. Several additional issues must be considered by the committee before it can draft this statement.

1. If no deliberate and corporate thought is given to this subject, some members will automatically assume that the goal is for the church to become as large as possible, while others will feel that the best thing is to top off at about three hundred members. If different members are quietly assuming different goals, sooner or later there will be open confusion and frustration.

2. If the church wants to become as large as possible, foresight must be used either to purchase adequate ground or else to locate and build in such a way that it is reasonably possible to sell in order to make a necessary expansion later.

   The goal of a large church will also necessitate a special approach to organization so that the church continues to be a living organism even when it is large. Churches must plan ahead to guarantee that the interpersonal relationships remain adequate for every member to feel that he is an important part of the church, no matter how large the membership has become. To delay implementing this kind of approach until the church is in danger of losing this sense of life and community is both foolish and disastrous.

3. If the church wants to limit its ultimate size, a program is necessary that will prepare the members in their personal commitment to participate in a mother-daughter program.[9] Along with this would be the necessity to handle the funds so that a well-determined concept of division of equity would be followed each time a daughter church was established. A corollary to this is that the amount and duration of any indebtedness adopted by the church which will become the mother church must be structured so that these financial obligations do not in fact prohibit a daughter church from coming into existence.

   Again, with this goal in mind, the mother church must be setting aside some funds to assist the daughter church when the time comes. Experience has shown that these facets can become emotional problems for the church that suddenly decides to establish a daughter church without these long-range preparations being actively processed.

Before deciding how large the church should become, the committee must take into consideration the general survey of its

---

9. See *The Birth, Care, and Feeding of a Local Church*, chapter 19.

community. The matter of ultimate size will be affected by the kind of community in which the church wants to serve. For instance, in a community in which homes sell for more than fifty thousand dollars, the community would generally expect it to become a large church.

Another facet of the community to consider is the mobility or transience of the residents. If the majority of the families move every three years or less, the church probably would have no choice but to plan on being a small or a medium-sized church.

This statement, like that about the church building, will of necessity be more general than the first three of the statements drafted.

Completion and Adoption of a Statement

The compilation of these five statements is the finished draft.[10] It is necessary to spend time studying the composite statement to be sure that no contradictions or confusions have developed in the course of making the separate parts.

It is suggested that these statements, like the principial statement, be adopted provisionally. After living with the two provisional statements for several months, formal adoption of the declaration of specific purpose can be accomplished.

---

10. Note: No example has been given of the application of the principle to the five factors of influence. Such a presentation would be too lengthy for the purpose of this book.

12
Developing a Congregation That's Alive in Christ

What is it that sets a congregation apart as one that is really being blessed by God? A congregation can have a excellent pastor, elders, and deacons, and draft an excellent statement of specific purpose, and yet be sick with the malady known as "dead orthodoxy." On the other hand, it can have meetings going all the time, with singing, testimonies, and unrestrained enthusiasm, and be sick with "shallow emotionalism." Nor is the healthy congregation that church which achieves the happy medium between these two extremes. If that's all it has accomplished, it has merely substituted another malady, "mediocrity," for one or the other of the original problems. What is needed is to be a congregation unwilling to settle for anything less than a daily experience of being alive in Christ!

The church that is alive in Christ is the one in which each member can declare as a tangible and continuous testimony that participation both as an individual and as a part of the corporate body is satisfying his responsibility to glorify God while providing the blessing of enjoying him. For the church to be "alive in Christ" demands that the pastor, the elders, the deacons, and the statement of specific purpose all demonstrate "aliveness" through the four functions every church has.

But how does this even begin to happen? Each of the four major contributing factors to every church's life—the pastor, the elders, the deacons, and the specific purpose of the church—must in and of themselves demonstrate being alive in Christ. (Yes, even a document, the specific purpose, must have this characteristic as a fundamental part of its makeup.) As each one makes this demonstration, the congregation can in turn be led and challenged to be alive in Christ. This chapter is designed to show the way these factors accomplish this.

Reexamine the four functions of a church as visualized in figure 1. Two of the functions are specific and need only a little

159

comment here. The work of the deacons is the major contribution enabling a church to have a ministry of mercy. Needless to say, the deacons should be serving as men aware that they have been called to an office which, in and of itself, is a high office. Therefore, their labor as deacons is something very much less than even "ministry" in its broadest sense if it does not show a close and rewarding personal walk with the Lord. Its value is not measured by the quantity of labor and money expended, but by the quality of ministry offered. The deacons' contribution, therefore, is directly proportionate to the "aliveness" of the deacons themselves.

The next, the function of worship, has primarily the pastor and the elders responsible for its oversight. In all churches, worship demands the contribution of the worshipers, to be sure. And the function of worship is fully prescribed in the Bible itself, even more than many today are apparently willing to admit. Creative contribution to worship, therefore, must mean participation in all the Bible-prescribed parts of worship in more contemporaneous ways, not the use of created substitutes for the parts of worship themselves. Consequently, to the function of worship, the contribution by the pastor and elders, and any others delegated to assist, must be the demonstration of "aliveness" in Christ.

The other two functions of the church need more detailed discussion here. They are "growth in grace" and "outreach." Since they are each much broader in scope than either the "ministry of mercy" or "worship," the best way to discuss them is to analyze their structures. It is only when the congregation understands and appreciates the structures of these two functions that it will be able to enjoy its own involvement without restraint and, further, will have a tool to measure the hand of God upon it through these four factors (the pastor, elders, deacons, and the specific purpose).

The scope of the following material is so broad that the direct relationship of the "aliveness" in Christ of the pastor, the elders, the deacons, and the specific purpose will often seem to have little effect on the "aliveness" of the entire congregation. This is a false conclusion, though at first glance it will seem true enough. In the ultimate analysis, "deadness" on the part of one or all these factors will stifle the "aliveness" of the congregation or will create such tensions that the church almost inevitably will either split or sink to a low common denominator of "aliveness in Christ" and continue just to exist. In the detailed discussion of the structure of the two remaining functions of the church, this truth will be presumed as undergirding the entire material presented.

160

One further word of explanation is necessary before proceeding to the detailed discussion. Many aspects of the structure of these two church functions are in themselves subjects worthy of detailed study. The Sunday School is one. Many of these aspects have been studied in depth and excellent textbooks have been written on them. Here I have attempted to relate the primary purpose of each to the life of the entire congregation so that the church might really be "alive in Christ." Consequently the reader will not find here a mini-textbook on each facet being discussed.

The Church Function: Growth in Grace

Figure 1, chapter 1, shows the three major components of growth in grace. This discussion will use each of them as a topic.

Instruction

Every church must have a ministry of instruction that literally has no end. In the Great Commission is the following phrase: "teaching them to obey everything I have commanded you." To take that command literally demands more time for its completion than all of eternity will provide. Little wonder, then, that the evangelical church can never finish teaching—instructing—even the older saints of God as well as the babes in Christ. Also, in the light of the definition previously given for teaching ("instruction in the knowledge of his faith and its practice unto discipleship") no one can go on in his Christian experience without himself being taught.

1. The Pastor's Preaching-Teaching Ministry

His preaching-teaching ministry per se. This has been dealt with in chapter 3. One facet of that discussion must be restated here for emphasis, namely, it is primarily the pastor's task to administer the teaching responsibilities of the church. This does not mean, of course, that he is expected to do everything himself. It does mean he carries the ultimate responsibility to see that everything necessary for teaching is in fact accomplished. Again, it does not mean he carries all by himself the full responsibility for the caliber and content of the teaching done in the name of the church. The pastor and elders who share the responsibility must regularly evaluate the teaching done in the name of the church. Since the goal is to accomplish discipleship, the fruit of the Spirit (Galatians 5:22-23) must be more and more evident in life after life.

Extent of teaching. Clearly, then, the teaching ministry of the church must be adjusted to communicate to and to challenge members of every age simultaneously. In a small church, this might be difficult. At least some of the teaching (possibly once a month?) must be adjusted to reach the age group least represented in the congregation.

Teacher training. It is the pastor's responsibility to see that the teachers are properly qualified and trained. He may delegate much of this work in a large church, but he cannot delegate the primary responsibility for the teachers' qualifications and training. Also, he must be careful that the ultimate responsibility is not usurped from him by a Director of Christian Education. Regardless of the professional acumen and personal faith of the D.C.E., the ultimate responsibility must indeed rest upon the pastor's shoulders, demanding some regular involvement by him. The matter of selection of personnel will be discussed later in this chapter; the pastor must be involved at that level too.

2. General Areas of the Instructional Ministry

The Sunday School. The Sunday School is the first thing most people think of when asked about instruction in their church. Yet many Sunday Schools are woefully lacking and might well be disbanded to bring God the greatest glory! The reason for this is the purposelessness of most Sunday Schools. Most of them believe that their purpose for existence falls into one of the following five categories:

(a) to entertain or baby sit children so that the adults may participate in the worship service without distraction;
(b) to evangelize;
(c) to teach doctrine and Bible to the children of the church— and, to some degree, to the adults as well;
(d) to instruct the entire family in the whole counsel of God;
(e) some combination of b, c, and d.

An assessment of these "purposes" is in order.

For the first, to call Sunday School a baby-sitting service is a travesty.

162

For the second, I have seen only one Sunday School really doing work of evangelism. The truth of the matter becomes evident when the Sunday School tries to answer the question: "If Sunday School exists to evangelize, where are the lost, week after week, who must be reached with the Gospel?" Also, when Sunday Schools declare themselves primarily concerned with evangelism, they imply that for all the years he attends, the pupil will be fed the same basic lesson every week. Since the child of God must be fed the whole counsel of God (whether he knows it or not!) if he is ever to grow into spiritual maturity, the majority of Sunday Schools that try to accomplish this purpose usually lose their children at the junior high school age.

The third expression of purpose has more merit to it than either of the first two, but it still leaves much to be desired. If such a Sunday School does at least this much very carefully and diligently, a tangible blessing will flow from it. But it is deficient as a reason for being because it does not consider the needs of the adults of the church worthy of much effort.

The fourth and fifth kinds of Sunday Schools are the most productive. Those dealing just with instruction to the Christian families may accomplish the most per Sunday, yet they tend to presume that everyone attending is already a Christian and so become tools in fostering the concept of "presumptive regeneration." A balance between evangelistic concern and solid teaching of the Bible and doctrine for everyone in the family is the best arrangement.

However, if a Sunday School does attempt to have a meaningful instructional ministry to everyone in the family, that program will have to be coordinated with the Summer Bible School curriculum, a churchwide family devotional program (if one exists), and all special teaching programs of the church, such as a pastor's communicants' class.

Finally, the actual purpose of the Sunday School must be an expression of the specific purpose of the church. It is toward this that the Sunday School should be oriented and by its standards that the Sunday School should be evaluated.

The Summer Bible School. Many churches have a DVBS (Daily Vacation Bible School). Some special, in-depth training such as this is valuable, but it does not necessarily have to be one that, even in its name, emphasizes the vacation aspect of the school.

Handwork should be at an absolute minimum, possibly limited to children of seven or younger. An attempt should be made at least to survey the Bible in classes for fifth through eighth graders, or their equivalent in departmental groups. Evangelism should be a strong thrust of the school but certainly not the entire purpose of it. Again, the curriculum should complement the Sunday School curriculum.

For those using a catechism, the Summer Bible School can be an invaluable tool to teach the catechism. It would be wise to have the Bible memory work be the proof-text support of the catechism itself.

Finally, there should be a teaching ministry by the pastor in the Summer Bible School. His ministry to the older pupils may well develop long-range relationships and consequences not possible any other way.

In recent years many churches have been conducting their Summer Bible School in the evening so that adults can participate as well.

Bible classes outside the church. Bible classes may be designed to accomplish several purposes. Before delineating them, a word of warning is in order concerning all Bible classes not related to the church. Throughout the book it has been stressed that the pastor-teacher plus the elders carry primary responsibility for what is taught to the congregation. Too often, sincerity coupled with enthusiasm is the ultimate source of authority for independent Bible classes and, as a result, heresies may spring from these classes to plague the church. On the other side of the coin, however, God has often used these classes to supplement (rather than merely complement) church ministries that have failed to "feed the lambs." The pastor must use the sincere and enthusiastic Bible teachers! But he should train them, encourage them, be a resource person to them, and occasionally sit down with them and evaluate their ministry.

Bible study classes. These are the usual kind of classes, most often simply studying a book of the Bible verse by verse. These classes often continue year after year. Care must be taken that they have a specific goal and are in fact accomplishing it or they may become a "habit," so to speak, and actually serve to drain off vital energy and ministry from other classes simply because no one is willing to "call it quits."

Bible classes for evangelism or growth for the babe in Christ. These classes usually last only a short time—one or two months. They often are conducted in the home of a church member who

164

invites neighbors or young Christians. Care must be taken not to presume the Bible is a book of magic to be used to accomplish conversion in these classes. Rather, the Bible must be related to the work of the Holy Spirit in inspiration and to the fact that it is God's revelation of himself.

These classes often use a topical rather than a book-of-the-Bible approach. Also, the material taught may be in printed lesson form, with the topic clearly enunciated, supporting Bible verses listed, and ample blank space for the student to fill in his understanding of each Bible verse.

Whatever teaching means is used, the teacher must be very careful not to become a slave to the tool and consequently be insensitive to the real needs of each member of the class.

Bible classes and book studies in order to answer specific problems. Every young Christian has a host of questions about God, the universe, the Bible, world history, and especially about his own walk of faith in the contemporary world. Most pastors tend to deal with these as individual problems and believe that their preaching and an occasional visit is sufficient to answer them. Usually this is just not so. Consequently, many folks just shove their questions to the back of their mind, sometimes to be haunted by them later in life or to become frustrated enough to go to someone else who will take the time to recognize that the person *and* his problem are important and will give him an answer. Often there are several people asking the same questions. If so, a special Bible study for several weeks is in order. If only one or two are asking, one very good way to deal with the situation is to lend the person a well-written book on the subject, give instruction in the format and distinctives of the book (a fifteen-minute visit at the most!) and return two or three weeks later to discuss the problem with him in the light of the reading he has done. Many of these problems can be handled this way in part or in whole by the elders.

Instructional mandates. Before leaving the area of general instructional ministries, four extremely important policies—mandates, if you will—must be stated. They cannot be ignored, or all the teaching effort expended will be useless or even destructive to the building up of the body of Christ.

1. The basis for all teaching is the Bible, the verbally inspired, infallible Word of God.
2. The Bible not men, documents and books, experiences, or

165

personal feelings—is the final authority for what the Christian believes and what he does.

3. The basic doctrines of the Bible are absolutely clear and discernible throughout the Bible. Other facets of the Bible are of immense value and importance but may not be absolutely crucial to the salvation and edification of God's children.[1] Care must be taken to make this distinction in order to avoid implying that those Christians disagreeing with the teacher on these minor points are second-rate.

4. The best commentary on the Bible is the Bible itself, and therefore all of the Bible must be brought to bear on each point to be made in a teaching situation.

3. Specialized Areas of the Instructional Ministries

This topic includes whatever is necessary to help and encourage the individual Christian constantly to be growing in spiritual maturity.

Individual tutelage. Mature members of the church, with the elders in the vanguard, should spend the time and love necessary to appreciate every young babe in Christ and give each one personal encouragement, insights, challenges, exhortations, etc. (1 Corinthians 12:21).

Removing blocks to interpersonal relationships. This ministry usually must be done by qualified professionals for the congregation. It is a specialized ministry, not to be confused with the work of the elders in dealing with discipline problems that may be blocking growth and interpersonal relationships. It is often used by the Holy Spirit to pour out special blessings "in the midst of the believers" in addition to blessing the individual believer himself.

Specialized teaching circumstances. Premarital counseling is a must for every church. What many churches and pastors fail to see is that premarital counseling must start long before young people get engaged. Actually, it must be a never-ending ministry of teaching and preparation to all the young people, year after year. Then, for a young person of the church who decides to be married,

---

1. For instance, the difference between the premillennarian and the amillennarian views.

additional, intensive premarital counseling should be conducted. This counseling ought to extend even to matters of finances. Possibly a team—pastor, elder, and deacon—should be used in conducting the work.

Another kind of specialized counseling is the ministry to each of the age groups in the church about their particular needs, areas of fulfillment, ways and means of sharing, and special dangers from worldly practices. This ministry will probably be to teenagers, to family units, and to senior citizens more than to the other age groups. No church is really developing the supply of one "ligament" to the other if this ministry is not vital. A major means of accomplishing this teaching is through camps, conferences, retreats, and workshops, which will be discussed later in this chapter under the topic of "Fellowship."

Another area of specialized teaching is that of relating the Bible and its teaching to the contemporaneous and controversial subjects of the day. It is a long-standing proverb that politics and religion don't mix, but it is probably an oversimplification. Certainly the church is not to be involved with the merits of one candidate for office as opposed to another, unless there is flagrant immorality or a major apostate position held by a candidate. And it should be a foregone conclusion that the church ought not to take sides on issues that are not germane to the purpose and standards of the church. But, having said that, the church must provide a forum for its people to discuss these issues in order to understand the immediate problems before the people in the light of the Bible. If people are talking and praying about issues at home, there should be some forum for them to find help from their church to better make up their minds about the issues. Three examples may help to clarify this point.

1. Years ago I was asked to vote in a national church meeting on the action President Truman took against General Mac Arthur in Korea. In retrospect, the discussion amounted to an exchange of ignorance. No one present was qualified to pass on advice, let alone judgment, on the matter. Actually, the specific issue before the church wasn't the business of the church, and consequently wasn't a proper subject for consideration by the church.

2. In another circumstance, the question of birth control was to be discussed. I brought qualified representatives of two points of view (it happened that one was a theological professor and the other was a practicing physician) to the dis-

167

cussion. Other points of view were also recognized and informally discussed. The final conclusion was that the pastor and elders gave general advice, with only those points made specific which reflected the Bible's revelation about various aspects of the topic. Handled this way, the subject was a proper one for church consideration.

3. I was confronted with the sensitive subject of the occult. After discussion, led by qualified personnel, a definite conclusion was reached, and categorically taught as well as defended (cf. James 4:6-8). (The conclusion, by the way, was to reject all "experimenting" with the occult, no matter how inconsequential the action might be, because of the tremendous power of Satan.) Again, this was a proper subject for church consideration.

The church must be dealing with the issues of contemporary life. But it must be careful to keep within the area of responsibility and to be authoritative and absolute only where it stands solidly on biblical principles. This particular area of instruction, although essential, must have the mature oversight of the pastor and elders to guide it.

Another specialized teaching tool is a good-quality library in the church, with an emphasis on periodicals and major theological texts. During the orientation for candidates for membership, the use of the library should be taught, not simply stressed. A word of warning is in order. Too often churches establish libraries, using primarily books left over from church members' personal libraries. This is a dangerous practice; a worthwhile library will reject some books as irrelevant, outdated, or too worn out. Acquisitions should be made by the church on a carefully determined policy and almost always by purchase.

Sanctification

Sanctification is the daily work of the Holy Spirit's grace enabling the Christian to overcome the flesh and walk in the Spirit. The discipline aspect of sanctification often comes to mind first, but it is only one part of growing in grace, albeit the most difficult part. There are very many more aspects that must be working throughout the organism, and even the organization, of the church at the same time. One of these is the matter of prayer and devotional life of the church.

1. Prayer and devotional life. The healthy church must have a strong prayer life. It is in the gracious interplay of prayer concern and love for one another that the "glue" of the church (each ligament supplying graces to the other joints—Ephesians 4:16) is most fully developed. Such things as church activities, the numerical growth of the congregation, and the deep involvement necessary to accomplish building programs are often accepted as satisfactory "glue," but these are deceptively sticky to say the least. The question that must be dealt with is how to develop a unified, God-blessed prayer base for the church family.

Several basic axioms add up to an answer. The first is that people must appreciate the need for prayer before they will pray. Involvement in community prayer life will not be accomplished by lecturing (or by verbal whippings from the pulpit). Nor can righteousness, sanctification, and prayer life be accomplished by legislation—rules—or by the carrot-on-the-end-of-the-stick approach of promised dividends if one participates. People are motivated when they feel personal need. Necessity will succeed where external pressure often destroys the very grace it is attempting to foster. And it must be remembered that people grow in this experience; true development of this grace will take time.

Another basic axiom is that the experience of powerful praying on the part of a church is directly proportionate to two conditions:

- A core of members of the church faithfully carrying on a deep and detailed community prayer concern for each other, for the rest of the church, for the witness of the church, for missions and missionaries, and for the pastor and officers of the church. As answers become evident to more and more members, demonstrating the work of the Holy Spirit, the prayer group will increase.
- A core of members of the church faithfully practicing personal and family devotions in their homes. These usually are the same people who meet for community prayer sessions each week. This experience of individual and family devotions makes very personal the need and value of prayer. As in the previous case, the results of God's work in individual lives becoming more and more evident is usually used by the Holy Spirit to excite others, especially when they are going through times of need themselves.

Pastors must be aware that new converts often have to be taught (by example in the home!) how to pray and how to conduct devotions if the church and the individual are to grow in these graces.

Another basic axiom is that the church must supply ample opportunity for its prayer and devotion core or other members to share God's blessings with the rest of the church. The "short testimony" time between hymns in an evening service is often used for this purpose. Many Christians question the validity of injecting this activity into a worship service, and there appears to be no overwhelming evidence that this procedure really motivates others to seek similar blessings in their long-range growth in grace. Possibly a better procedure would be to have the testimony carefully prepared (which certainly can be done without losing the force of the testimony), perhaps with the help of the pastor or an elder if necessary, for use as a specific part of the worship service.

The testimony need not be merely the most evident way in which God providentially answered prayer or preserved life. It could include the effects of God's working in all the aspects of one's life and in the lives of others. Ideally it would lead the listening church into deep prayer concerns for the future consequences of the events shared.

Another means of sharing God's answers to prayer and the providential preserving of his own is to set apart special services (such as Thanksgiving Day services) for the purpose.

Still another means of sharing can be accomplished by having the pastor and elders, who should be aware of much of God's working in the lives of the members, personally bring people who need to hear the way God has worked together with people in whom God has worked. I was once faced with a member of my church attempting to commit suicide as a result of deep emotional depression. Earlier I had helped another person find the grace of God to overcome in the same situation and to find great power and peace in prayer. This person had never made his previous deep depression public, but he had agreed to help anyone else he could. I brought these two men together and thus became a bridge for in-depth sharing of blessings. The end of the story, by the way, is that God again saw fit to give grace to overcome this problem. The one helped came to see his need in the light of God's grace instead of his own frustration. God blessed him as a consequence of his experience, and now both men have made themselves available to help anyone else who may come to this point of desperation.

A final axiom is that the church corporately should regularly recount God's blessings and seek to show the relationship of these blessings to the prayer concern of the people of the church. The responsibility to see that this is done is the pastor's or officers' or both.

2. Specialized counseling situations. This subject was introduced as part of the ministry of the pastor as a deacon (see chapter 4). Here it is sufficient simply to point out several specialized areas in which it must be applied in order to assure growth in grace by the church. These areas include marital counseling, alcoholism and drug abuse, family breakdowns, inroads of worldly temptations, financial problems, and problems dealing with the basic purpose and meaning of life itself.

Much of this can and should be done by the elders of the church, although the pastor, of course, carries the ultimate responsibility for this ministry.

Fellowship

Fellowship is a major need of the church. It has a strange characteristic, however: its growth is not proportionate to the degree of effort specifically expended to develop it but to the love and need each member begins to feel for the other members of the church. There is a place for name cards for visitors and for "ice breaker" programs for visitors, especially in the first few visits to the church; but these efforts must only begin, not constitute, the ways and means of fellowship. Actually, the "glad-handing" of a newcomer to church should only make it possible for him to see he is wanted and needed for himself and that the church has that which he needs. If the program of "ice-breaking" for new members does not lead to this conclusion within one or two months, the newcomer will probably be a dropout. Fellowship must be a by-product of every facet of the church's life—including worship and especially participation in the sacraments.

It is amazing—the value in fellowshiping about the meal table. It is not an accident that the Lord mentions his saints joining with him in the marriage *feast* of the Lamb. In the light of this it is significant to note in how many churches, even large churches, members are spending most of the Lord's Day together, and eating together. (Of course, special provision must be made to accommodate this activity so that it does not become a violation of the Sabbath.)

One of the basic tools for developing fellowship in the church is to provide ways and means for the families of the church to visit together and enjoy each other as families. An extension of this tool is to have the families of the church invite visiting families into their homes early in their experience with the church.

Constructing the church building provides a specialized opportunity to know and appreciate one another, thus developing deep fellowship. Men's and women's meetings, couples' groups, and the like, also provide such opportunities.

Special weekend retreats and camping experiences do this as well. Some churches provide initial in-depth orientation primarily through weekend retreats. In other churches, such experiences are regularly organized for one or another cross-section group of the church so that at least every second or third weekend some such retreat is going on.

It is apparent that fellowship is a product of vital interchange of lives, a consequence of time provided to accomplish a given purpose.

Two other areas must be mentioned. Participation in preparing and presenting special music as a part of the church's worship is a special source of growth in fellowship for those able to be involved. However, fellowship itself can become the prime purpose for participation in this ministry. When it does, the ministry is no longer properly oriented to the church, at least for that individual, and usually becomes a divisive experience.

The other area is participation in denominational activities if the church is part of a denomination or association.

A serious warning concerning worship and fellowship has been issued in chapter 2 of *The Birth, Care, and Feeding of a Local Church*. It is sufficient here simply to mention the danger of permitting the experience of fellowship to become the sole yardstick by which growth in grace is evaluated. It can never be such a norm!

Outreach

Outreach is the other church function whose structure is to be described in this chapter. Reference should be made to figure 1, chapter 1, to see the major components of the function.

Evangelism

In chapter 10, much has already been said about evangelism. Here a basic fact must be stressed. Too often evangelism is conducted on a very shallow premise. Some are content with the concept that evangelism is simply "spreading the seed." Others relate evangelism simply to the way in which a church grows. In fact, evangelism for the church of God is its outreach that enables the lost, as God calls his own to himself, to be born into the spiritual and visible family of God—the church. Converts to a vacuum is anything but biblical.

With this in mind, it is sufficient simply to point out that there are many ways for the church to participate in evangelism. No one way is the total answer, of course.

Finally, a church does not really become an evangelistic church simply because evangelistic messages are regularly preached from the pulpit. Only when the members themselves become involved will the church really be evangelistic. And that will not happen simply by instructing members in what to say and do. Each member must be encouraged to demonstrate his faith as best he can, regardless of the extent of his biblical knowledge, and most of them must be given actual in-the-field experience and training.

Missions

Missions is extending the church.[2] It does not place foreign in opposition to national situations. Both aspects of the work are involved with developing churches. The so-called foreign missionary does not go to be a foreigner pastoring a native church. If he goes to Africa, for instance, his calling is to "disciple-ize" as well as evangelize so that there will be an African pastor and African elders and deacons in an African church. Although culture and distance do make it necessary to attack the problem differently in different places, the goal at home and abroad is the same—establishing churches.

The way a local church is involved with missions at home and abroad is the key to developing this aspect of outreach. When a church member occasionally hears about a missionary and his field, occasionally is given pertinent data about which to pray, the missionary and his ministry remain to a large degree an appendage to the vital purpose of his church experience. And he seldom can do more than maintain a sincere concern, probably a wholesome sympathy, for the missionary. However, when the church develops

2. See chapter 1, *The Birth, Care, and Feeding of a Local Church,* regarding the Great Commission of Matthew 28.

173

a deep involvement in missions and missionaries as part of its very purpose of existence, in every age group of the church simultaneously and continuously, most church members will have the opportunity to laugh with the missionary, cry with the missionary— even die a little when the missionary dies. In effect, the family of the church has been extended to include the missionary as part of itself, and the church begins to empathize with him. This attitude is significant because it is always easier for a family to support one of its own with prayer and finances, and even to go to help him, than it is for non-family-related people to do so. Thus, a church becomes mission minded.

One of many practical ways to help introduce empathy and revolutionize a church's missionary involvement is to make a church missionary conference a family affair instead of a public meeting conference. To do so, the missionary would probably lead the church in worship on the Lord's Day (note: not substitute for worship data and stories about his field!). Then on each night of the week he would be in a different home of the congregation. That family would open their home to others. The missionary would speak—no more than thirty minutes—and then would enter a free-flowing question and discussion period about any aspect of his ministry that seemed apropos.

Finally, mention must be made of the "Faith-Promise" plan now used by many evangelical churches. The essence of the plan is to promise a firm financial support that is clearly beyond tithing. By faith, a promise is made for this additional giving. There have been many successes from this program. However, if the program is geared just to one facet of the church (for instance, foreign missions), the danger exists that the church may become overbalanced in its emphasis. And it really doesn't do much to foster empathy as opposed to mere sympathy.

Community Concern

The evangelical church probably cannot and perhaps should not become deeply involved in some community concerns beyond those already discussed in chapter 8. This is not to say that individual members should not. Actually, they very much should.

Some activities not referred to in chapter 8 in which the church can become involved are community projects in response to natural disasters, and hospital and retirement projects that have an evangelical base. In addition, the community may occasionally

174

make a justifiable request for the use of the building for one or another of its secular projects, such as using the church basement for a polling place at the time of an election.

This concludes the discussion of the structure of these two functions. However, several major presumptions have been made throughout and must be defined and discussed to complete the chapter.

Selecting and Training Personnel for the Task

In almost every church there is the problem of getting enough people to do the work. This problem has another even more significant one related to it, namely, whether the church and its total ministry are of major importance to its members. This second problem cannot be solved by forcing people into service with threats or anguished pleas. It is solved by providing every member and friend the opportunity to share his gifts with the others and in turn to be blessed by the others. It must be solved on the basis of need motivating commitment which in turn motivates participation. This pattern must be the formula throughout the overall ministry of the church, not just for the specific "job" to be accomplished at the moment. Thus the entire church takes a responsibility toward each new friend and member from the point of view of needing to share each other's gifts.

Accomplishing this sharing also requires the initial assessment by the elders of the spiritual maturity and gifts of the new members. This data will make it possible at least to know the general areas in which members (and often faithful friends as well) are qualified and possibly gifted.

A warning is needed to the very small church. With only a few people, each person must often do many jobs. Extreme care must be taken to:

- set priorities of immediate importance among the goals and admit that some things just will not get done, at least for a while
- set priorities of necessary preparation time among the goals to be accomplished, so that no work is done without adequate preparation
- reevaluate, at least once a quarter, in an attempt to employ others, particularly newcomers, to spread the load
- insure that each one serving in any way is emotionally com-

175

mitted to relinquishing his work, even to less qualified people on occasion, for the most complete use of all the people [3]

In training personnel, the basic responsibility for biblical and doctrinal material rests on the shoulders of the pastor-teacher (Ephesians 4:11-12). As the church grows, this ministry must grow by sharing the work with others, either with the elders themselves or with those authorized by the elders.

However, in the area of pedagogy, the pastor and elders almost always need professional help, at least when the work begins to grow. There must be some continual efforts to provide this specialized training for new recruits and to upgrade the techniques of those already serving.

Corporation, Finances, and Building Programs

Very little needs to be said here about the church corporation, finances, and building, since they are dealt with at length in *The Birth, Care, and Feeding of the Local Church*.[4] A biblical emphasis that must be stressed here, however, is that the physical and financial matters of the church are not "nonspiritual" matters. Paul, in speaking of gifts one Christian may have and another may not have, makes a fundamental assertion that cuts across every aspect of creation and life. In 1 Corinthians 4:7, he says: "What do you have that you did not receive?" Gifts, and even life itself, are ours only by the grace of God! Paul equates the spiritual and financial involvement of believers again in 2 Corinthians 8. "But just as you excel in everything—in faith, in speech, in knowledge, in complete earnestness and in your love for us, see that you also excell in this grace of giving" (v. 7); "for you know the grace of our Lord Jesus Christ, that though he was rich, yet for your sakes he became poor, so that you through his poverty might become rich" (v. 9). No church may dare permit a dichotomy to exist—spiritual matters on the one hand and physical and financial matters on the other. In proportion to the stress placed on their unity, the mechanics of the corporation's business will be in focus with the universal and the specific purpose of the church.

---

3. *Organization and Leadership in the Local Church,* by Kilinski and Wofford (p. 57 ff), presents a "Membership Profile" and discussion proposing a systematic approach to this problem.
4. See chapters 11, 14, and 18.

Two practical guidelines should also be noted here:

1. Open, constant, and easily understood reporting of all financial matters must be made to the church.
2. All special activities undertaken by the church normally should be self-sustaining.

Conclusion

There is no guarantee that every local church, following the proposals detailed in this chapter, automatically will be a congregation that is alive in Christ. However, these structures, as related to the entire church function, provide the means by which the aliveness of the church can become a wildfire for everyone. Yet it must be pointed out again that unless the pastor, elders, deacons, and specific purpose are alive in Christ, the church won't be. However, in God's marvelous grace, more than once he has chosen to use Spirit-filled laymen, through the structure of these church functions, to "turn on" the pastor and other leaders. When this happens, the appropriate response is: "Hallelujah!"

Appendices

Goal Setting Demonstrated

Each church should have an ultimate goal: to be that which the Bible declares a true, visible church should be. Further, the very existence of this ultimate goal implies the natural corollary that the church has subordinate goals that will reflect the major areas of its ministry. Before stating these subordinate goals and using some of them to demonstrate goal setting, an additional factor of church life must be considered; namely, that the life of the pastor and his family is woven into the life of the church. This factor must be taken into account or the goals set will be theoretical at best, and this must be done even though pastors occasionally leave and even though the life-style of the new pastor and his family may require entirely new goals.

The number of circumstances in which goal setting could be used by a pastor and church is almost limitless. The areas where it is absolutely essential are limited and easily definable. These areas and their major subdivisions will constitute the basic outline from which one point will provide an exercise in goal setting.

I.   The Pastor's Family Responsibilities:

   A. Living as pastor and husband and father.
   B. Determining the role of the minister's wife in the life of the church.
   C. Determining the role of the minister's children in the life of the church.
   D. Determining with the church a salary figure that is neither too low nor too high (which, in effect, balances the people's responsibility with the pastor's spiritual commitment, while permitting him to integrate his commitment with his responsibility to provide for his family for the present and the near future and for his retirement).
   E. Determining the ways and means of applying the family commitment necessary to live with the salary given by the church.

II.   The Pastor's Ministry:

   A. Determining the specific responsibility to the congregation in serving as its prophet and resource person.

B. Determining the best use of personal gifts to accomplish his ministry.
C. Determining a schedule for each day which will permit the necessary time for devotions, family, study, pastoral duties, planning, etc.
D. Determining the proper proportion of his time to be given to advanced study (if any).
E. Determining the proper time and emphasis to give to community activities.
F. Determining the proper time and emphasis to give to denominational (or, in some cases, inter-church) activities.

III. Development of the Church:

A. Developing, refining, and using the specific purpose for the congregation in each of the factors of influence of each church.[1]
B. Developing the internal strength of the church (with special emphasis on the church as an organism and also on the relationship between the organism and the organization of the church).
C. Developing the external witness of the church (with special emphasis on evangelism and missions).
D. Developing a daughter church or at least local church extension.
E. Developing a building program.

An example will be taken from Part I of this outline:
The Pastor's Family Responsibility—as a husband and a father.

Since every family is a unique group and every member of the family is a unique individual, at best I will only illustrate goal setting in this area in general terms; each pastor must, of course, set his own goals. Goal setting for such a thing as the responsibility to be a good husband and father could easily be by-passed, either on the premise that the Bible is perfectly clear on the subject or that it is so subjective an area that no goal is even remotely possible. The fact is, however, that many ministers are married, yet living a divorce (since neither he nor his wife want to admit openly the failure of their marriage), a situation that could have been avoided if both had agreed on just what they were anticipating out of their marriage and ministry.

The way to begin goal setting is to establish the prerequisites to the problem and thus at least determine a sense both of direction and boundary. The first prerequisite of a goal is that it should be biblical. Almost any concise survey of the Bible will easily show most of the content of this prerequisite. For instance:

• a husband is to love his wife "just as Christ loved the church" (Ephesians 5:25);

---

1. See chapter 11.

- husbands ought to love their wives "as their own bodies. He who loves his own wife loves himself" (Ephesians 5:28);
- husbands should "be considerate as [they] live with [their] wives and treat them with respect as the weaker partner" (1 Peter 3:7);
- a husband is the head of the household and therefore of his wife—"Wives submit to your husbands. . . . For the husband is the head of the wife . . . " (Ephesians 5:22-23);
- a husband is the head of the household and therefore of his children—"Children, obey your parents in the Lord, for this is right. . . . Fathers, do not exasperate your children; instead bring them up in the training and instruction of the Lord" (Ephesians 6:1, 4).

The next prerequisite is that the goal must be measurable. In order to set a goal in the area of his role as a husband and father, the pastor must make subjective assessments. But however difficult they are, he *must* make them and must constantly reevaluate them. One measurement must be of love. The pastor is married because God caused him and his wife to love each other, and love is a real thing even though it is almost impossible to put into words. The husband must constantly be satisfied deep in his heart that his love for his wife is growing and that her love for him is growing, too. In the spiritual concern that he has for his wife and his children, he must again use subjective judgment. In all honesty he must admit that he can indeed determine something of the degree of spiritual maturity each of his family enjoys and whether it is increasing or decreasing. As the head of the household, he must be aware daily of practical expressions of their spiritual concern and commitment and of its growth or decline, such as individual participation in family and in public worship, facing temptations and overcoming them by the grace of God, even if doing so means "going it alone" instead of with "the gang."

Finally, goals are to be reasonably attainable. The husband-father-pastor will have some decisions to make in order to assure reasonableness in his goal. Achieving growth of love between husband and wife and growth of spiritual maturity in each family member will take a great deal of time, and under occasional stressful circumstances may even take an inordinate proportion of his time. And when the normal demands of the pastorate are added, it almost always seems impossible to achieve these three facets of life simultaneously. The answer must lie in quality of involvement rather than quantity of time spent on each. Having accepted this concept, the pastor must determine what the difference is between quantity and quality involvement for each relationship and consider his goal attained only if he can honestly measure quality involvement. For instance, he may have to conclude that he cannot be with his children in all the junior league ball games, but that he will always be enough abreast of his children that he can easily recognize and talk through with them each new activity or influence that occurs in their lives. Attaining this goal may demand some kind of prearrangement with church officers for freedom to adjust his schedule in order to respond to the needs and opportunities when they arise for his wife, his children, and his whole family.

In summary, a minister and his wife should live consciously with the biblical relationship of personal love and of family headship, with the willingness to assess regularly whether love is indeed growing, and to anticipate that quality, not quantity, will be used as evidence that their goal is being achieved.

Already the goal has taken specific form. The pastor, as a husband and a father, must seek to experience the composite conclusions of these prerequisites as his goal. This example is now almost complete.

When this goal is subjected to the special pressures involved in the pastorate, it becomes evident that even in the area of his personal life the pastor will have to make priority decisions. For instance:

- he must be available to shepherd his congregation when they need him
- he must have time for personal study
- he must be able to spend extra time with church duties during certain parts of the church calendar year (i.e., the Christmas season)

I do not believe it would be meaningful to develop all the facets of these three kinds of priorities, since no specific case is at hand. To illustrate the use of priorities it may help to point out one or two solutions that I applied in my own case. Because I was out just about every night, while my children were young I came home by 4:30 P.M. each day, had an early family supper, had ample time for devotions and for personal time with each child separately, and was gone by 7:00 or 7:30 P.M. Also, I did my studying at home, not in the church study, so that I could pick it up at any free time.

Now, when the goal has been set and the priorities adopted, a small step of faith must be taken each day. Willingness to change the "usual" to accomplish the goal is a step of faith. Commitment to keep at it, in spite of the workload, is also a step of faith. The anticipated result of this goal is that the minister will have a family that knows God. There are tremendous consequences of living with this goal; it is a hard fact of life that God occasionally permits a pastor to be disappointed in the lives of his children, especially in their teenage years. However, if the pastor has set his goal and its priorities and he has lived with it, small step of faith by small step, he will be able to differentiate between parental guilt and parental concern. A pastor can continue an effective ministry with any degree of parental concern that God permits him to bear. But in the light of Paul's list of qualifications for the office of pastor-teacher ("He must manage his own family well and see that his children obey him with a proper respect"—1 Timothy 3:4), he will not be able to continue an effective ministry at all if he is burdened with parental guilt!

This illustration needs one more note of practical application before it is complete. The pastor must communicate with his church about his conclusions in this matter at least to the extent that his officers are aware of his goal and the basic priorities he has set relative to it, and are sympathetic to it. Also, the pastor must seek their help, especially any wisdom they can offer and any creative ideas they can supply, and such information comes only through viable communication.

Appendix B
How to Brainstorm

The purpose of brainstorming is to engage a group of people in exploring a single issue, without restraining their imaginations, in an attempt to develop new and creative ideas with which to deal with the issue.

There are several keys to making brainstorming sessions a success:

1. thoughts and ideas should be called out (often shouted out!) as they come to mind, regardless of their apparent feasibility or acceptability;
2. no discussion of any comment is permitted;
3. "chain-reaction" comments (a series of comments, each a contribution on its own, which are the consequences of a new idea just voiced) should be encouraged;
4. all participants are urged to continue to call out ideas as often as they can;
5. each contribution is recorded as it is made. (Possibly two or three secretaries are needed, each taking half or a third of the comments on a rotating basis.)

There is one concept which is fundamental to a successful brainstorming session, and it must be agreed to by all the participants. It is that each participant should contribute to the session spontaneously and without restraint. This means that:

1. each participant must be willing to identify with the issue at hand as imaginatively as possible;
2. he must be uninhibited in voicing his thoughts as they occur, regardless of the customary courtesy and deferences to "chain of command" relationships normally in force between the participants;
3. he must be free to respond to the issue being brainstormed without regard to the so-called image that he is normally expected to project.

Some guidelines are needed to assure a productive brainstorming session:

1. a leader must be in charge and have sufficient authority to start the session and to keep it from deteriorating;

186

2. a precise statement of the issue must be given by the leader before the session starts;
3. the issue must be communicated sufficiently well for the participants to give evidence that they comprehend the meaning of the statement;
4. it is wise to have at least one trial brainstorming on a simple and totally unrelated subject (often humorous) for a short time if the participants are unfamiliar with the experience;
5. the leader ought to be able to start the session by contributing at least one or two seed ideas;
6. the leader must keep the session from the pitfall of clichés. If a cliché is given, the leader may do well to ask the participant to restate the thought in his own words;
7. the leader must keep any kind of divisive bias from taking advantage of the brainstorming session to gain a platform of respectability. In order to do this, the leader must make the participants aware, before starting the session, what bias-prone themes are almost sure to come up. Further, he must instruct the participants that he will be looking for the bias-prone comments to emerge in bits and pieces, that he will not prejudge any individual contribution, but will terminate the session if it appears that a divisive bias is in fact being projected.

The initial assessment of the brainstorming session normally is done by the participants almost directly after the session itself. The objective of this assessment is twofold:

1. to arrange the results of the brainstorming session in at least a general order of priority so that the experience of brainstorming is still an influence on setting the order of priority. (Note: at this point the priority listing ought not reflect to any great extent the feasibility or acceptability of any proposal.)
2. to assign committees (at least for the high-priority suggestions) to do initial research on the proposals made.

Appendix C

A Sample Questionnaire and Schematic Survey

of the Procedure of Drafting the Statement
of Principle of the Specific Purpose for a Church

SAMPLE QUESTIONNAIRE
(C-1)

(INSTRUCTIONS)

(a) Do not discuss these questions with anyone.
(b) Husbands and wives should each submit their own answers, again without discussing them first.
(c) Do not sign your return.
(d) Express yourself at length.
(e) Read through the entire questionnaire before answering any of it.
(f) Mail your answer directly to the Committee on Assessment.

1. Describe in detail two ways in which you are specially blessed in the church.
2. Describe in detail two ways in which you are disappointed in the church.
3. What two parts of a standard worship service mean the most to you? Why?
4. Have you contributed to the spiritual welfare of any other Christian in the church within the past four weeks? How?
5. What is the difference between this church and an evangelical church (such as _____) in our neighborhood? What is your reaction to this difference? Why?
6. In a *short* paragraph define the doctrine of this church.
7. In a *short* paragraph define the government of this church.
8. In a *short* paragraph describe the responsibilities of the officers of this church.
9. Describe the kind of people to whom this church could most easily communicate the Gospel.
10. How should this church present the Gospel to the lost?
11. Must this church have land soon, and a building soon thereafter, to

188

survive? or, How should the entire church plant be used to bring the greatest glory to the Lord?

12. What is there about this church that demonstrates the presence of the living God?

EXPLANATION OF THE QUESTIONNAIRE
(C-2)

A. Questions 1, 2, and 3 supply the data with which to answer the question: What is necessary for the congregation to be fulfilled in their worship and experience?

B. Questions 4 and 12 supply the data with which to answer the question: What is necessary for the congregation to demonstrate that they indeed serve the living God?

C. Questions 9, 10, and 11 supply the data with which to answer the question: What is necessary for the congregation successfully to communicate the Gospel to their community?

D. Questions 5, 6, 7, and 8 supply supporting data for all the above questions plus an indication of the congregation's appreciation of just what their church is, whether or not it is needed, and whether or not the majority of members feel it is well unified.

COLLECTING THE DATA
(C-3)

The data will come from four basic sources:

A. Answers to the questionnaire.

B. Results from any brainstorming sessions.

C. Results from an in-depth survey[1] of the general and the ecclesiastical circumstances of the area.

D. Statement of preconceived goals prepared by members of the congregation.

REFINEMENT OF THE SCHEMATIC SURVEY

I. For an Embryonic Church

A. During the first phases of development[2] the entire concept of the specific purpose should occasionally be discussed.

---

1. See *The Birth, Care, and Feeding of a Local Church*, chapter 5.
2. Ibid., chapter 3ff.

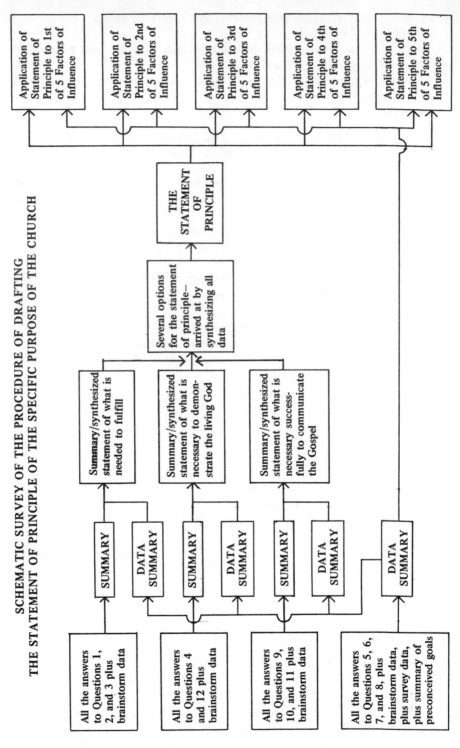

SCHEMATIC SURVEY OF THE PROCEDURE OF DRAFTING
THE STATEMENT OF PRINCIPLE OF THE SPECIFIC PURPOSE OF THE CHURCH

Application of Statement of Principle to 1st of 5 Factors of Influence

Application of Statement of Principle to 2nd of 5 Factors of Influence

Application of Statement of Principle to 3rd of 5 Factors of Influence

Application of Statement of Principle to 4th of 5 Factors of Influence

Application of Statement of Principle to 5th of 5 Factors of Influence

THE STATEMENT OF PRINCIPLE

Several options for the statement of principle—arrived at by synthesizing all data

Summary/synthesized statement of what is needed to fulfill

Summary/synthesized statement of what is necessary to demonstrate the living God

Summary/synthesized statement of what is necessary successfully to communicate the Gospel

SUMMARY

DATA SUMMARY

SUMMARY

DATA SUMMARY

SUMMARY

DATA SUMMARY

DATA SUMMARY

All the answers to Questions 1, 2, and 3 plus brainstorm data

All the answers to Questions 4 and 12 plus brainstorm data

All the answers to Questions 9, 10, and 11 plus brainstorm data

All the answers to Questions 5, 6, 7, and 8, plus brainstorm data, plus survey data, plus summary of preconceived goals

B. A general concensus of a specific purpose should be adopted anu recorded. (Care must be taken not to allow these discussions to become the major concern of the church.)
C. Shortly before the church assumes its full responsibility of self-government, or at least after it has been in existence fifteen or more months, these general conclusions should be reviewed and expanded. The questionnaire (Appendix "C-1") should be used as a guide to be sure that all facets of the concept have been involved.
D. This study should be drafted into summary to be used as part "A" (Appendix "C-2") of the four basic sources upon which a statement of principle of specific purpose is drafted.
E. In small groups, much of the synthesizing (Appendix "C-3") can be done by meeting as a "committee of the whole."

II. For Churches of Two Hundred or More

A. The pastor and elders should enlist the participation of key personnel of the church to constitute a "congregation" to develop the programs as described in the text.
B. Committees should be structured from among this group to do this development and carry it to completion.
C. During the process of developing the statement and then of applying it, regular reports must be made to the entire church.
D. Also, during this process, channels of communication between the church and the "congregation" doing the work must be established. The "congregation" must seek contributions of ideas, etc., and must be sensitive to them.

Appendix D
The Consultant

Before looking for a consultant, the church must first understand what his task is, and then what characteristics and attitudes he must have in order successfully to complete his job.

QUALIFICATIONS OF THE CONSULTANT

The major characteristics and prerequisites to look for in choosing a consultant can be listed.

First and foremost, the pastor, elders, and people of the church drafting the declaration[1] must have the confidence that the consultant is a man of God, committed to the Bible as the Word of God written, inspired in the original; to Jesus Christ as God in the flesh, the only Savior of man; and to the universal purpose of the church, the reconciliation of God and man rather than only reconciliation among men.

The consultant must be a man with considerable experience in church work, and this work must bear the stamp of God's blessing. Much of his value will of necessity stem from a wealth of experience in the practical inner working of a church's life.

The consultant must be of such a disposition that he naturally makes people feel at ease. This is necessary so that the people will be both encouraged to express their personal opinions and confident that their expressions will be handled with discretion.

The consultant must be experienced in discerning between the major and minor aspects of a given situation, particularly in the context of the contemporary religious scene and its complex interactions.

The consultant must be known to have some experience in using a sanctified imagination; in other words, he must be creative.

The consultant must be familiar with and committed to the concepts developed in this presentation of a declaration of specific purpose for each church.

---

1. Or, statement of principle of the specific purpose for a church.

192

NOT THE PASTOR

The pastor of the congregation drafting the declaration ought not be the consultant. The desire to have him serve in this capacity is natural and often very strong. For instance, once the church appreciates the need for a declaration, it is often tempted to have the pastor direct the process so that it can "get the show on the road," rather than taking the necessary time to find an outside person to serve as the consultant. A greater temptation to do this exists when it is evident that the pastor is indeed qualified to serve as a consultant.

To understand why the pastor cannot be used as the consultant, the impact of the program must be appreciated. In the first place, drafting the declaration is a spiritual exercise of the heart, in which the most basic ideas and practices of the church members, including the pastor and his family, are examined. In the second place, after the declaration is adopted, the pastor must be the leader in the weeks and months of spiritual confrontations that follow as the declaration is applied to one area after the other of the church's life.

Inevitably these confrontations experienced by the congregation will either be stepping stones of faith so that they see and claim new victories for the Lord, or stumbling blocks of frustration that could split the church. If there exist the slightest grounds for accusations that the pastor has not been personally involved in a spiritual exercise of his own heart or that he has been manipulating to achieve a declaration of his own ambitions, the church member facing a spiritual confrontation will not respect the pastor as objective and consequently reject his leadership. Once the pastor has lost the respect of his flock, he will not be able to serve his people successfully.

FINDING THE CONSULTANT

It is difficult to find a professional consultant in this work. However, many pastors and elders, particularly in churches of the same doctrinal position, can do the work of the consultant for churches other than their own congregations. The consultant should not be from a church whose ministry is contiguous with or overlaps the geographical bounds of the church seeking to draft the declaration. In a large metropolitan area the consultant could easily be from another part of the city, but in a rural area or in a small town or city, he could not be from the same location.

Appendix E

BIBLICAL QUALIFICATIONS FOR ELDER
(A Composite of 1 Timothy 3 and Titus 1)

MUST HAVE A CHRISTLIKE CHARACTER	MUST HAVE A CHRIST-CENTERED FAMILY	MUST HAVE BIBLICAL AND DOCTRINAL KNOWLEDGE	MUST HAVE SOME GIFTS
Above reproach Temperate Prudent Respectable Hospitable Not addicted to wine Gentle Uncontentious Free from love of money Good reputation with those outside church Not accused of dissipation or rebellion Not self-willed Loving what is good Sensible Just Devout Self-Controlled	Husband of one wife Manages own household well Having children who believe	*Not a new convert Holding fast the faithful word	Burdened to taking ruling responsibility Prudent Apt to teach Exhort in sound doctrine Refute those who contradict

*Implication is that a mature knowledge of Bible and doctrine exists.

194

BIBLICAL QUALIFICATIONS FOR DEACON

MUST HAVE A CHRISTLIKE CHARACTER	MUST HAVE A CHRIST-CENTERED FAMILY	MUST HAVE BIBLICAL AND DOCTRINAL KNOWLEDGE	MUST HAVE SOME GIFTS
Men of dignity Not double-tongued Not addicted to much wine Not fond of sordid gain First tested—to be beyond reproach	Wives: Dignified Not malicious gossips Temperate Faithful in all things Husbands of one wife Good managers of their children and their households	Holding to mystery of the faith	Full of the Spirit and of wisdom